Essential Elements of English Grammar

A Guide For Learning English

William Dixon

iUniverse, Inc.
Bloomington

Essential Elements of English Grammar

A Guide For Learning English

iUniverse books may be ordered through booksellers or by contacting:

iUniverse
1663 Liberty Drive
Bloomington, IN 47403
www.iuniverse.com
1-800-Authors (1-800-288-4677)

Because of the dynamic nature of the Internet, any web addresses or links contained in this book may have changed since publication and may no longer be valid. The views expressed in this work are solely those of the author and do not necessarily reflect the views of the publisher, and the publisher hereby disclaims any responsibility for them.

Any people depicted in stock imagery provided by Thinkstock are models, and such images are being used for illustrative purposes only.

Certain stock imagery © Thinkstock.

ISBN: 978-1-4502-8460-8 (sc)
ISBN: 978-1-4502-8458-5 (ebook)

Printed in the United States of America

iUniverse rev. date: 1/20/2011

Contents

Foreword

<u>Simple Tenses</u>   Pages

Present..1 - 8

Past..9 - 18

Future..19 - 21

Simple Verb Tense Review...22 - 23

<u>Progressive Tenses</u>

Present Progressive..24 - 33

Past Progressive...34 - 39

Future Progressive..40 - 42

Progressive Tenses 43

Present, Future, or Future Progressive...44

Progressive Tense Review 45

Progressive Verb Tense Review..46

Simple and Progressive Verb Tense Review...47

<u>Perfect Tenses</u>

Present Perfect ....48 - 53

Past Perfect ....54 - 57

Future Perfect ....58 - 61

<u>Perfect Progressive Tenses</u>

Present Perfect Progressive ....62 - 66

Past Perfect Progressive ....67 - 71

Future Perfect Progressive ....72 - 75

Review/Part I 76

Title Page – Part II 77

Spelling Rules for Past Tense Regular Verbs..78

Common Regular Verb Forms 79

Common Irregular Verb Forms ....80 - 81

Passive Voice ....82 - 91

Modal Auxiliaries...92 - 106

Conditional Sentences ....107 - 110

Wish ....111 - 114

Tag Questions..115 - 117

Too 118

So...119

Either..120

Neither 121

Too, So, Either, Neither – Review...122 - 125

Problem Verbs ....126 - 131

Gerunds and Infinitives ....132 - 141

Participial Adjectives ....142 - 143

Review/Part II ....144 - 145

Answer Key/Part I ....146 - 155

Answer Key/Part II ....156 - 161

Dear students and teachers,

Thank you for using my book. I hope you enjoy it. This series is made up of two books. Book I covers the twelve verb tenses of English and other topics related to the use of verbs (passive voice, auxiliary verbs, and conditional sentences). Book II covers parts of speech (noun, adjectives, adverbs, and prepositions).

My purpose in writing these books is I believe that grammar is a key component for learning to use the English language well. Grammar teaches how to use a language correctly by following rules. These books are designed to be used by students in a classroom setting or by an individual student in self-study. The answer key at the back of the book is provided so that students can check their answers.

For students, I have used a variety of vocabulary words to challenge you. As you study, I recommend that you have a dictionary nearby to look up any new words so that you can increase your vocabulary as you learn grammar.

For teachers, the contents of this book can be expanded to include writing and conversation activities. For example, if you are covering the past tense, you can ask the students to write sentences in the past tense, or use a conversation activity that focuses on the past tense.

Good luck,

William Dixon
August 2010

Present Tense – To Be Verb

Use the present tense when an action happens every day, all the time, or as a regularly scheduled event. The present tense form of the "to be" verb (am, is, are) is used alone with no other verbs.

I am   You are

He is   We are

She is   They are

It is

A very common sentence pattern is <u>subject</u> + <u>to be verb</u> + <u>adjective</u>.

Examples: The house is big.
           The boys are thirsty.
           I am sleepy.

Directions: Put the correct form of the "to be" verb (am, is, are) in the blank.

1.   Linda _____ seven years old.

2.   I _____ tired.

3.   Bob and Mary _____ married.

4.   She _____ at home right now.

5.   The dog _____ black and brown.

6.   We _____ very hungry.

7.   Elsy _____ from Mexico.

8.   You _____ happy.

9.   He _____ ready to go.

10. The house _____ clean.

Present Tense – To Be (Negative Form)

Use am, is, are + not for the negative form.

is not = full form

isn't = contraction

The full form and the contraction are both correct and have the same meaning. Most native English speakers use the contraction more often than the full form, but both forms are correct.

I am not / I'm not	You are not / aren't
He is not / isn't	We are not / aren't
She is not / isn't	They are not / aren't
It is not / isn't	

Example: Glenn is not here.
Glenn isn't here.

Directions: Use the negative form of the "to be" verb in the blank.

1.   This plate _____ clean.

2.   Jose _____ at work.

3.   They _____ friends anymore.

4.   The house _____ pretty.

5.   Her hair _____ black.

6.   Most stores _____ open on Christmas.

7.   You _____ old.

8.   Maria _____ married to Pablo.

9.   I _____ a doctor.

10.   These plates _____ clean.

Present Tense – To Be (Question Form)

To make a present tense question with the "to be" verb, put <u>am</u>, <u>is</u>, or <u>are</u> in front of the subject.

Example: <u>Harry is</u> angry at his boss.   <u>Is Harry</u> angry at his boss?

Directions: Change the following sentences into questions.

1.   Linda's pencil box is blue.

2.   The dogs are friendly.

3.   I am stubborn.

4.   Glenn is three years old.

5.   Alma and Bertha are from Mexico.

6.   The music is too loud.

7.   Elizabeth and Richard are married.

8.   The food at that restaurant is delicious.

9.   They are hungry.

10.   I am always late.

Spelling Rules for Present Tense Action Verbs (Third Person)

In the present tense, the third person (he, she, it) takes a different spelling than I, you, we, they.

Add s to most verbs for the third person subject.

Examples: I eat grapefruit every morning.

He eats grapefruit every morning.

Add es to verbs that end in ch, sh, s, x, z.

Examples: watch / watches

wash / washes

kiss / kisses

mix / mixes

buzz / buzzes

Add s to verbs that end in y when the letter before y is a vowel (a, e, i, o, u).

Examples: buy / buys

play / plays

employ / employs

For verbs that end in y, when the letter before y is a consonant, change the y to i and add es.

Examples: cry / cries

study / studies

For the verbs do, go, and have, the third person form is irregular.

Examples: do / does

go / goes

have / has

Present Tense – Action Verbs

Use the present tense when an action happens every day, all the time, or as a regularly scheduled event. Action verbs in the present tense are used alone and not with the present tense form of the "to be" (am, is, are) verb.

I eat	He eats
You eat	She eats
We eat	It eats
They eat	

Notice that the third person (he, she, it) has a different ending than the other subject pronouns.

Spelling Rule #1: If an action verb ends in o, x, ch, sh, s, or z, add es to the verb.

Spelling Rule #2: If an action verb ends in y with a consonant before the y, change the y to i and then add es.

Examples: Jose goes to work every day.
            She studies at the library every night.

Directions: Use the present tense form of the verb in parentheses.

1.   David _____ (live) in Houston.

2.   They _____ (live) in San Antonio.

3.   The dog _____ (want) more food.

4.   The printer _____ (need) more ink.

5.   I _____ (like) this song.

6.   He _____ (wash) his car every Saturday.

7.   They _____ (go) to church on Sunday morning.

8.   You _____ (buy) a lot of cookies every week.

9.   She _____ (ride) her bike to school.

10. Gerald _____ (talk) about his problems all the time.

Present Tense – Action Verbs (Negative Form)

To make action verbs negative in the present tense, use <u>do</u> + <u>not</u> or <u>does</u> + <u>not</u>. Do not use am, is, are with an action verb in the present tense.

Example: I <u>am not live</u> in Ohio. (incorrect)
　　　　　 I <u>do not</u> live in Ohio. (correct)

I do not / don't like
You do not / don't like
We do not / don't like
They do not / don't like

He does not / doesn't like
She does not / doesn't like
It does not / doesn't like

<u>Do not</u> is the full form and <u>don't</u> is a contraction. Both are correct, but native English speakers use the contraction more often.

Example: Glenn <u>works</u> at a refinery.
　　　　　 Glenn <u>doesn't **work**</u> at a refinery.

The action verb in the negative form is the simple form of the verb.

Directions: Change the following sentences to the negative form.

1.　　Miguel has a new baby.

2.　　She drinks coffee every morning.

3.　　I have a headache.

4.　　They eat at a restaurant every Saturday night.

5.　　We watch television every night.

6.　　Sheila speaks Chinese.

7.　　Joanie wants a cheese pizza.

8.　　Sebastian drives a red truck.

9.　　You work at a shoe store.

10.　　Linda walks to school every day.

Present Tense Verbs (Negative Form)

Is not is the full form, and isn't is a contraction. Both forms are correct, but contractions are more commonly used by native speakers than the full form.

I am not = I'm not	I do not live = I don't live
He is not = He isn't	You do not live = You don't live
She is not = She isn't	We do not live = We don't live
It is not = It isn't	They do not live = They don't live
They are not = They aren't	He does not live = He doesn't live
You are not = You aren't	She does not live = She doesn't live
We are not = We aren't	It does not live = It doesn't live

A contraction cannot be made from am not.

Example: Positive = I am a teacher.   Negative = I am not a teacher.

Example: Positive = I live in Colorado.   Negative = I don't live in Colorado.

Example: Positive = He lives in Colorado.   Negative = He doesn't live in Colorado.

*Notice that the verb **lives** changes to **live** in the third person negative.*

Directions: Change the following sentences from positive to negative.

1. Jim likes his new job.

2. Pedro is married to Daniela.

3. He exercises every day.

4. Art has a beard.

5. Melinda and Joe work together.

6. Dave lives in an apartment.

7. The washer is broken.

8. The tires are new.

9. They have three children.

10. The keys are lost.

Present Tense – Action Verbs (Question Form)

To make a present tense question with an action verb, use <u>do</u> or <u>does</u> + <u>subject</u> + <u>the simple form of the action verb</u>.

Examples: They live in California.   <u>Do they live</u> in California?
He lives in Utah.   <u>Does he live</u> in Utah?

Directions: Change the following sentences into questions.

1.   Emilio speaks Portuguese.

2.   The class studies grammar every day.

3.   I have two children.

4.   Sara and Todd run three miles every morning.

5.   Karl eats oatmeal for breakfast.

6.   Cesar has a new car.

7.   Many people go grocery shopping on Saturday afternoon.

8.   Sheila wants a cup of coffee.

9.   You like this kind of music.

10.   Avery washes her car once a week.

Past Tense (To Be)

When a condition was true yesterday, last night, last week, or at sometime in the past, use the past tense.

I was

He was

She was

It was

You were

We were

They were

Examples: The weather <u>was</u> cold last night. ***The weather = It***

Bob and Mary <u>were</u> tired from their trip. ***Bob and Mary = They***

*Typically, <u>was</u> is used with subjects that are singular (one) and <u>were</u> is used with subjects that are plural (two or more). However, **you** can be singular or plural, but <u>were</u> is the only correct answer.*

Directions: Use either was <u>or</u> were to complete the sentences.

1. Ron _____ sick last week.

2. Pete and I _____ friends many years ago.

3. They _____ absent yesterday.

4. The banks _____ closed on Thanksgiving.

5. I _____ tired last night.

6. You _____ nice to my friends.

7. The dogs _____ in the backyard.

8. The chair _____ broken three days ago.

9. She _____ in Mexico last month.

10. Dinner _____ delicious!

Common Regular Verb Forms

For regular verbs, the simple past form and the past participle form are the same.

Examples: I <u>wash</u> my car every Saturday. (Present)
I <u>washed</u> my car last Saturday. (Past)
I <u>have</u> already <u>washed</u> my car. (Present Perfect)

1.	act	26.	decide	51.	listen
2.	add	27.	destroy	52.	live
3.	advise	28.	dry	53.	look
4.	agree	29.	end	54.	love
5.	answer	30.	enjoy	55.	miss
6.	apologize	31.	enter	56.	move
7.	argue	32.	erase	57.	need
8.	ask	33.	explain	58.	obey
9.	bake	34.	finish	59.	open
10.	beg	35.	fix	60.	own
11.	behave	36.	follow	61.	paint
12.	belong	37.	happen	62.	park
13.	borrow	38.	hate	63.	plan
14.	breathe	39.	help	64.	play
15.	brush	40.	improve	65.	pull
16.	call	41.	include	66.	push
17.	carry	42.	join	67.	reach
18.	change	43.	jump	68.	seem
19.	clean	44.	kick	69.	smile
20.	close	45.	kiss	70.	spell
21.	complain	46.	kill	71.	start
22.	cough	47.	knock	72.	stay
23.	cry	48.	laugh	73.	stop
24.	chew	49.	learn	74.	study
25.	dance	50.	like	75.	talk

Spelling Rules for Past Tense Regular Verbs

Regular verbs in the past tense end in <u>ed</u>. Regular verbs, unlike irregular verbs, follow spelling rules for past tense conjugation.

For verbs that end in e, add <u>d</u>.

Example: like / liked

For one-syllable verbs that end in consonant – vowel – consonant, double the final consonant and add <u>ed</u>.

Example: plan / planned

For two-syllable verbs that end in consonant – vowel – consonant with pronunciation stress on the second syllable, double the final consonant and add <u>ed</u>.

Example: admit / admitted

An exception to the rule is never double <u>w</u> or <u>x</u>.

Examples: chew / chewed

        mix / mixed

For verbs that end in y, if the letter before the y is a vowel, add <u>ed</u>.

Example: pray / prayed

For verbs that end in y, if the letter before the y is a consonant, change the y to i and add <u>ed</u>.

Example: deny / denied

For all other regular verbs, just add <u>ed</u> to make the verb past tense.

Example: park / parked

Common Irregular Verb Forms – Page 1

<u>Simple</u>	<u>Simple Past</u>	<u>Past Participle</u>
be	was, were	been
become	became	become
begin	began	begun
bite	bit	bitten
blow	blew	blown
break	broke	broken
bring	brought	brought
build	built	built
catch	caught	caught
choose	chose	chosen
come	came	come
cut	cut	cut
do	did	done
draw	drew	drawn
drink	drank	drunk
drive	drove	driven
eat	ate	eaten
fall	fell	fallen
feed	fed	fed
feel	felt	felt
fight	fought	fought
find	found	found
fly	flew	flown
forget	forgot	forgotten
get	got	gotten / got
give	gave	given
go	went	gone
grow	grew	grown
have	had	had
hear	heard	heard
hit	hit	hit
hold	held	held
keep	kept	kept
know	knew	known

Common Irregular Verb Forms – Page 2

Simple	Simple Past	Past Participle
leave	left	left
lend	lent	lent
light	lit	lit
lose	lost	lost
make	made	made
meet	met	met
pay	paid	paid
quit	quit	quit
read	read	read
ride	rode	ridden
ring	rang	rung
run	ran	run
see	saw	seen
sell	sold	sold
send	sent	sent
set	set	set
sing	sang	sung
sink	sank	sunk
sit	sat	sat
sleep	slept	slept
speak	spoke	spoken
spend	spent	spent
stand	stood	stood
sweep	swept	swept
swim	swam	swum
take	took	taken
teach	taught	taught
tear	tore	torn
tell	told	told
think	thought	thought
throw	threw	thrown
understand	understood	understood
wear	wore	worn
win	won	won
write	wrote	written

Past Tense (Action Verbs)

There are two forms of past tense verbs, regular and irregular. Past tense regular verbs end in ed, and past tense irregular verbs do not end in ed.

Examples: work – worked   tie – tied   study – studied
            eat – ate   find – found   fly – flew

Directions: Supply the past tense form of the verbs in parentheses.

1.   I _____ (buy) a car five years ago.

2.   Melinda _____ (study) math yesterday.

3.   They _____ (play) soccer at the park.

4.   Fidel _____ (write) a letter to his brother today.

5.   The little boy _____ (break) his new toy.

6.   Manuel _____ (wear) a suit to his job interview.

7.   Elvira _____ (graduate) from high school in 1987.

8.   Keith _____ (get) a job last week.

9.   She _____ (drink) two cups of coffee earlier.

10.   Ted _____ (wash) his car last Saturday.

Past Tense (To Be and Action Verbs/Negative Form)

I was not/wasn't	I did not/didn't go
He was not/wasn't	He did not/didn't go
She was not/wasn't	She did not/didn't go
It was not/wasn't	It did not/didn't go
You were not/weren't	You did not/didn't go
We were not/weren't	We did not/didn't go
They were not/weren't	They did not/didn't go

Do not mix a "to be" verb with an action verb in the past tense.

Example: He <u>was not</u> <u>work</u> last week. (Incorrect)
            He <u>did not/didn't</u> <u>work</u> last week. (Correct)

Directions: Change these past tense sentences to the negative form.

1.   Alex was sick yesterday.

2.   We worked in the yard last Saturday.

3.   Bud went to Las Vegas in December.

4.   They ate spaghetti for dinner last night.

5.   We were married in 1995.

6.   You saw my wife at the grocery store.

7.   I needed aspirin for my headache.

8.   Mario had two cups of coffee this morning.

9.   We reached our goals.

10.   Elsy and Guillermina were absent four days ago.

Past Tense (Questions)

Form questions in the past tense of "to be" by placing the verb <u>was</u> or <u>were</u> before the subject.

Example: They were absent yesterday.
           Were they absent yesterday?

Directions: Change the following past tense sentences to questions.

1.   Sara was a good tennis player.

2.   Keith was a bad employee.

3.   They were friendly with each other.

4.   Friday was a very nice day.

5.   Martha and Adrianna were from Mexico.

6.   The exercises in Chapter One were easy.

7.   I was busy on Thursday night.

8.   Felix and his wife were compassionate with the young woman.

9.   Both windows were closed.

10.   We were upset by the terrible news.

Past Tense (Questions)

Form questions in the past tense (to be) by placing the verb <u>was</u> or <u>were</u> before the subject.

Was I sick yesterday?
Was he sick yesterday?
Was she sick yesterday?
Was it sick yesterday?

Were you sick yesterday?
Were we sick yesterday?
Were they sick yesterday?

Form questions in the past tense (action verbs) by placing <u>did</u> before the subject and using the action verb in the simple form.

Did I go yesterday?
Did he go yesterday?
Did she go yesterday?
Did it go yesterday?

Did you go yesterday?
Did we go yesterday?
Did they go yesterday?

Directions: Change the sentences to the past tense question form.

1. Arturo had a mustache last year.

2. Margarita went to Canada in June.

3. Luis was a doctor in El Salvador.

4. Julie made several mistakes on her test.

5. We were surprised to see Julio at the party.

6. Gerald was correct about his predictions for 2008.

7. Larry ran five miles yesterday morning.

8. Pamela built a new house in 2006.

9. Arnoldo lost his job at the warehouse.

10. Lupe was late for her shift at the hospital last night.

Past Tense Review

Directions Part I: Answer the questions in the positive form.

Examples: Were you thirsty?
Yes, I was thirsty.

Did Carl work today?
Yes, Carl worked today.

1.   Did the students work well together?

2.   Did Patricia wear a black dress to the funeral?

3.   Were the teachers angry about the boss' decision?

4.   Was he at work yesterday?

5.   Did Felix get a new watch for Christmas?

6.   Did Lisa go to the dentist this morning?

7.   Was the food hot?

8.   Was the class ready for the quiz?

9.   Did Maria seem upset?

10.   Did you break my pencil?

Directions Part II: Answer the questions in the negative form.

Examples: Were you thirsty?
No, I wasn't thirsty.

Did Carl work today?
No, Carl didn't work today.

Future Tense

There are two forms of the future tense, <u>will</u> and <u>going to</u>.

I will go	I am going to go
You will go	You are going to go
He will go	He is going to go
She will go	She is going to go
It will go	It is going to go
We will go	We are going to go
They will go	They are going to go

You can use either <u>will</u> or <u>going to</u> for predictions. You can use only <u>going to</u> for a prior plan. You can use only <u>will</u> for something that indicates a willingness to do an action.

Directions: Use <u>will</u> or <u>going to</u> in the following sentences. If the sentence is a prediction, then <u>will</u> and <u>going to</u> are both correct.

1. The Houston Astros _____ (win) the World Series next year.

2. My family _____ (go) to Florida next summer.

3. The telephone is ringing. I _____ (answer) it.

4. Pete _____ (retire) in two years.

5. Someone is ringing the doorbell. I _____ (get) the door.

6. Sally _____ (wash) her car on Sunday afternoon.

7. It _____ (rain) on Monday evening.

8. Paul and Lisa _____ (sell) their house and move to Ohio.

9. Don't worry! I _____ (help) you change the flat tire.

10. We _____ (deposit) my paycheck in the bank tomorrow.

Future Tense (Negative Form)

<u>Will</u>

I will not / won't leave
You will not / won't leave
He will not / won't leave
She will not / won't leave
It will not / won't leave
We will not / won't leave
They will not / won't leave

<u>Going To</u>

I am / I'm not going to leave
You are not / aren't going to leave
He is not / isn't going to leave
She is not / isn't going to leave
It is not / isn't going to leave
We are not / aren't going to leave
They are not / aren't going to leave

Directions: Change the following sentences to the negative form.

1. The Houston Texans will win the Super Bowl next season.

2. Bob is going to teach tennis next June.

3. Peter is going to buy a new car next December.

4. I will help you next weekend.

5. They are going to go to San Antonio on Saturday.

6. We will win the lottery very soon.

7. Betty is going to go to the doctor Thursday.

8. You will pick Hannah up at school on Friday.

9. Nannette will follow us to the store.

10. You are going to be sorry about the decisions that you are making.

Future Tense (Questions)

Will
Will I take?
Will you take?
Will he take?
Will she take?
Will it take?
Will we take?
Will they take?

Going To
Am I going to take?
Are you going to take?
Is he going to take?
Is she going to take?
Is it going to take?
Are we going to take?
Are they going to take?

Directions: Change the following sentences to questions.

1.   The U. S. economy will recover soon.

2.   William is going to start his own business next year.

3.   They are going to sign the contract tomorrow.

4.   The meeting will be over by two o'clock.

5.   I am going to move to Bay Oaks in three years.

6.   Melinda is going to fly to Los Angeles on Monday.

7.   Steven is going to study business in college.

8.   Vanessa will become a very good tennis player.

9.   Raquel is going to begin piano lessons in April.

10. The professor will start his lecture at 7:00.

Simple Tense Review – Present, Past, and Future

Directions Part I: Answer the following questions in an affirmative manner.
Do not change the verb tense.

Examples: Does Lisa take a shower every morning?
Yes, Lisa takes a shower every morning.

Were you at the party on Sunday?
Yes, I was at the party on Sunday.

1.   Are they going to work in the garden this weekend?

2.   Will it rain on Friday?

3.   Do Penelope and Kris have a cat?

4.   Does it smell like wet dog in Bud's bedroom?

5.   Did Natasha speak to the class?

6.   Were they happy to see Jack?

7.   Did you watch the speech on television last night?

8.   Is Julie going to be the new boss?

9.   Is Julie the new boss?

10.   Will you do me a favor?

Directions Part II: Answer the questions in a negative manner. Do not
change the verb tense.

Example: Does Lisa take a shower every morning?
No, Lisa does not / doesn't take a shower every morning.

Were you at the party on Sunday?
No, I was not / wasn't at the party on Sunday.

Simple Verb Tenses (Present, Past, and Future) – Sentence Correction

Directions: Correct the mistakes in the following sentences.

Example: Javier will goes to the store for you. (Incorrect)
                 Javier will go to the store for you. (Correct)

1.   The students taked a test last Friday.

2.   What are you do after class tomorrow?

3.   Lindsay and Catherine wasn't happy with the test results.

4.   Where was you go yesterday?

5.   I didn't told Martha your secret.

6.   Mrs. Smith isn't drive a blue car.

7.   You going to work late on Saturday.

8.   Is Cynthia work at a pizza restaurant?

9.   The printer don't have enough ink to make copies.

10.   Are you going to get a haircut a few days ago?

Spelling Rules for Present Participle (Progressive) Verb Form

*The present participle verb form ends in **ing**. This form is used for progressive verb tenses. To change a verb from the simple form to the progressive form, follow these spelling rules.*

If a verb ends in e, drop the e and add ing.

Example: come / coming

If a verb ends in ee, keep the final e and add ing.

Example: flee / fleeing

If a verb has one syllable and ends in consonant – vowel – consonant, double the final consonant and add ing.

Example: run / running

If a verb has two syllables, ends in consonant – vowel – consonant, and the second syllable is stressed in pronunciation, double the final consonant and add ing.

Example: admit / admitting

An exception to this rule is never double w or x.

Example: blow / blowing
             mix / mixing

If a verb ends in ie, change the ie to y and add ing.

Example: lie / lying

For all other verbs, just add ing.

Example: cry / crying

Present Progressive Verb Tense

Use the present progressive tense to show that an action is happening right now or at the current time.

Examples: Sheila is taking a nap right now.

   Alexis is living in Galveston.

   Jim and Dale are working overtime this week.

Form the present progressive by using the present tense form of the "to be" verb (am, is, are) with the present participle form (ing) of the main verb. The main verb is usually an action verb.

I am studying   You are studying

He is studying   We are studying

She is studying   They are studying

It is studying

Directions: Use the present progressive verb tense in the blanks.

1.   Alex _____ (fight) a cold.

2.   The Smith family _____ (live) in China.

3.   Please be quiet! Ann _____ (listen) to the radio.

4.   The students _____ (take) an exam.

5.   The company _____ (pay) all of our bills.

6.   Janet _____ (argue) with Gloria.

7.   I _____ (tie) my shoelaces.

8.   Dick _____ (run) at the park right now.

9.   Hugo and Paul _____ (play) golf today.

10.   Linda _____ (ride) her bicycle.

Progressive and Stative Verbs

Some verbs have a stative meaning. These verbs describe conditions that exist. When a verb has a stative meaning, it is not used in the progressive tense.

Some verbs can have a stative and a progressive meaning. When a verb has a progressive meaning, it describes an action.

Feel is in both categories. Feel in the stative form expresses an opinion. Feel in the progressive form expresses physical well-being.

Examples: I <u>feel</u> that the U. S. economy will recover next year. (opinion)
Carla <u>is feeling</u> sick. (physical well-being)

Stative	**Stative and Progressive**
appreciate	appear
believe	be
belong	cost
care	doubt
contain	feel
desire	forget
dislike	have
envy	imagine
exist	include
fear	look
feel	mean
hate	remember
hear	see
know	smell
like	taste
look like	think
love	want
need	weigh
owe	
own	
possess	
prefer	
realize	
recognize	
seem	
understand	

Progressive and Stative Verbs

Directions: Use the stative or progressive form of the verb in parentheses to complete each sentence.

1. I _____ (know) the answer to your question.

2. Rosa _____ (have) a great time at this party.

3. That book _____ (belong) to Alicia.

4. Paulina has a headache. She _____ (need) some aspirin to relieve the pain.

5. I _____ (recognize) that woman. She was my first English teacher many years ago.

6. Arnoldo _____ (owe) me ten dollars.

7. The first-aid kit _____ (contain) alcohol pads, band aids, a pair of scissors, and mosquito repellant.

8. The teacher _____ (talk) to his wife on the phone.

9. Chris and Paul _____ (feel) ill.

10. Dave _____ (think) about the answer to the math problem.

Present vs. Present Progressive

Use the present tense when an action happens every day, all the time, or as a regular event. Use the present progressive tense when an action is happening right now or at the current time.

Examples: I <u>play</u> basketball every Sunday afternoon. (Present)

            I <u>am playing</u> basketball right now. (Present Progressive)

Directions: Use the present tense <u>or</u> the present progressive tense.

1.   George _____ (watch) television right now.

2.   Dave _____ (watch) television every night.

3.   I usually _____ (go) to the grocery store on Saturday morning.

4.   I _____ (go) to the store now.

5.   She always _____ (eat) cereal for breakfast.

6.   Sergio _____ (wear) a suit today.

7.   It _____ (rain) right now.

8.   It _____ (rain) on average 100 days a year in Houston.

9.   Ed _____ (live) in California.

10.   Look! The dogs _____ (chase) a squirrel.

Present or Present Progressive

Directions: Use the present tense or the present progressive tense.

Examples: Louis is taking a nap right now. (Present Progressive)

Louis takes a nap every afternoon. (Present)

If the present tense should be used, clue words such as always, usually, and every are used to indicate the frequency of an action.

1. Angelica _____ (read) a book.

2. She _____ (read) a book every month.

3. Fidel and Elvira _____ (travel) to Mexico twice a year.

4. Betty _____ (wash) her car now.

5. She _____ (wash) it every weekend.

6. When Ed takes a shower, he _____ (sing) to pass the time.

7. Vanessa _____ (take) piano lessons.

8. Chase always _____ (play) soccer on Saturday morning.

9. Please be quiet! The students _____ (try) to concentrate.

10. My father usually _____ (cut) the grass on Monday.

Present Progressive (Negative Form)

I am not/I'm not talking
He is not/isn't talking
She is not/isn't talking
It is not/isn't talking

You are not/aren't talking
We are not/aren't talking
They are not/aren't talking

Directions: Change the sentences to the negative form. Some of the sentences are present tense, and some of the sentences are present progressive tense.

Examples: Larry <u>has</u> a part-time job. (Positive)
            Larry <u>does not/doesn't have</u> a part-time job. (Negative)
            David <u>is shopping</u> for a new car. (Positive)
            David <u>is not/isn't shopping</u> for a new car. (Negative)

1.   Angelica is reading a book.

2.   She reads a book every month.

3.   Fidel and Elvira travel to Mexico twice a year.

4.   Betty is washing her car now.

5.   She washes it every weekend.

6.   Eddie likes country music.

7.   Vanessa is taking piano lessons.

8.   Raquel plays soccer on Saturday morning.

9.   The students are concentrating on their work.

10.   My mother is eighty years old.

Present Progressive (Questions)

Am I writing?   Are you writing?
Is he writing?   Are we writing?
Is she writing?   Are they writing?
Is it writing?

Sometimes, the present progressive is used to express a future action. However, a future time must be used to avoid any confusion.

Examples: Sandra <u>is taking</u> a test <u>next month</u>. (Present Progressive)
                  Sandra <u>is going to take</u> a test <u>next month</u>. (Future)

Directions: Change the following sentences to question form.

1.   You are learning grammar in your English class.

2.   Sheila is beating Tim in their chess game.

3.   Leroy is wearing a gray suit to his job interview tomorrow.

4.   Deborah is cleaning the table.

5.   Chris and Roxanne are watching a movie in the den.

6.   We are meeting with a lawyer this afternoon.

7.   Joe's brothers are serving in the U. S. Navy.

8.   Our neighbors are selling their house.

9.   The boss is attending a conference in Dallas next week.

10.   Cynthia is leaving next Friday.

Present Progressive (Questions)

Directions: Change the following sentences to questions. Some of the sentences are present tense, and some are present progressive tense.

Examples: Jan is meeting with her boss. (Present Progressive)
Is Jan meeting with her boss?

Misty takes two vitamins every morning. (Present)
Does Misty take two vitamins every morning?

1.   You are going to the store today.

2.   They are renting a house in Clear Lake.

3.   Felix is changing a flat tire.

4.   Bertha is answering an e-mail from her sister.

5.   Rosalinda and Harriet are working at an elementary school.

6.   Mirna works at a daycare center.

7.   Mindy is from Vietnam.

8.   Yolanda has two dogs.

9.   The teacher likes Mexican food.

10.   The soda machine in the hallway is working now.

Present or Present Progressive (Questions)

Directions Part I: Answer the following questions in the positive (affirmative) form. Some of the questions are present tense, and some of the questions are present progressive.

1. Are you studying for the GED?

2. Does Luis wear glasses?

3. Are they in a big hurry?

4. Is Margarita wearing a red jacket?

5. Does Nadia have long hair?

6. Is Leticia at home?

7. Do you have children?

8. Are the students taking a test?

9. Do you like fast-food?

10. Is she nervous about her upcoming wedding?

Directions Part II: Answer the questions in the negative form.

Past Progressive Verb Tense

I was sleeping	You were sleeping
He was sleeping	We were sleeping
She was sleeping	They were sleeping
It was sleeping	

Use the past progressive with the past tense to show that the progressive action was in progress before the past tense action.

Example: I was sleeping *when the phone rang*.
          When the phone rang, I was sleeping.

When the phone rang is a time clause. If a time clause comes at the beginning of a sentence, a comma is used to signal the end of the time clause and the beginning of the main clause.

Directions: Use the past progressive form of the verb in parentheses.

1.   They _____ (eat) lunch when they saw Jim.

2.   It _____ (rain) when I left work.

3.   When you called, Henry _____ (take) a nap.

4.   A fire destroyed their home while they _____ (travel) in Poland.

5.   Ted fell as he _____ (get) into his truck.

6.   Ed _____ (live) in Canada when he got married.

7.   Gustav fell while he _____ (climb) a ladder.

8.   We didn't go to the zoo because it _____ (rain).

9.   Lynn _____ (study) while Anita cooked dinner.

10. Sara _____ (talk) when the teacher arrived.

Past vs. Past Progressive

Use the past progressive verb tense to show that the progressive action was in progress before the past tense action.

Example: I <u>was sleeping</u> when the telephone <u>rang</u>.

I was sleeping	You were sleeping
He was sleeping	We were sleeping
She was sleeping	They were sleeping
It was sleeping	

Directions: Use the past progressive or the past tense form of the verb in parentheses.

1. They _____ (eat) pizza for lunch yesterday.

2. It _____ (rain) three days last week.

3. Hugo _____ (take) a nap every afternoon when he was a child.

4. A flood _____ (ruin) their carpets.

5. Ted _____ (get) a new truck two months ago.

6. Linda _____ (play) golf when it started to rain.

7. I _____ (take) a walk when I smelled smoke.

8. I _____ (drive) on the freeway when I witnessed an accident.

9. While Hugh _____ (shop) at the mall, he ran into an old friend.

10. Elvira _____ (study) French when the doorbell rang.

Past Progressive (Negative Form)

I was not/wasn't working   You were not/weren't working
He was not/wasn't working   We were not/weren't working
She was not/wasn't working   They were not/weren't working
It was not/wasn't working

> Directions: Change the sentences to the negative form. Do not make the past tense verb negative, only the past progressive verb.

1. Roger <u>was studying</u> at the library last night.

2. When his wife called, Emilio <u>was working</u>.

3. On June 26, 2008, I <u>was living</u> in Japan.

4. You <u>were talking</u> after the test began.

5. The children <u>were lying</u> to their mother.

6. Sue <u>was swimming</u> in the pool when her nose started to bleed.

7. Bert <u>was waiting</u> at a stoplight when another driver hit his car.

8. When it started to rain, Bertha <u>was playing</u> in the park.

9. Snake <u>was riding</u> his motorcycle when the police officer stopped him.

10. Pat <u>was watching</u> a movie when his wife came home.

Past Progressive - Negative Form (#2)

Use the past tense to show that an action began and ended in the past. Use the past progressive tense to show that an action was in progress at some time in the past.

Examples: We <u>went</u> to the park yesterday. (Positive)
We <u>did not</u> / <u>didn't go</u> to the park yesterday. (Negative)

We <u>were renting</u> a house in 1995. (Positive)
We <u>were not</u> / <u>weren't renting</u> a house in 1995. (Negative)

Directions: Change the following sentences to the negative form. Some of the sentences are past tense, and some are past progressive tense.

1. Dave <u>was taking</u> a shower when the fire alarm went off.

2. Jose <u>left</u> a bottle of water in his classroom.

3. Shelly <u>bought</u> ten boxes of Girl Scout cookies.

4. At four o'clock on Saturday afternoon, I <u>was mowing</u> my yard.

5. Felix <u>was feeling</u> well last night.

6. Felix <u>felt</u> well last night.

7. The food at the Japanese restaurant <u>was</u> good.

8. Paula <u>read</u> two books last month.

9. Paula <u>was reading</u> a book when Hugo got home from work.

10. Homer and Lynn <u>were</u> at his sister's house last Friday night.

Past Progressive (Question Form)

Was I talking?   Were you talking?
Was he talking?   Were we talking?
Was she talking?   Were they talking?
Was it talking?

Directions: Change the following sentences to questions. Do not change
the past tense verb, only the past progressive verb.

Example: Nelson was arguing with Karen when they left.
            Was Nelson arguing with Karen when they left?

1.   Sharon was writing an essay when the electricity suddenly went out.

2.   Theodore and Sandy were getting off the school bus when we drove
      by.

3.   When the war started, Dale was living in Iraq.

4.   Sophia was eating her lunch when the boss came.

5.   Natasha was talking to Joseph when he had a heart attack.

6.   They were having a good time when Charles showed up.

7.   When you telephoned, Robert was eating dinner.

8.   The boys were playing basketball in the driveway when Mindy
      arrived.

9.   Hilda was traveling in Greece on September 11th, 2001.

10.   A police officer was questioning a witness when two detectives
      arrived.

Past vs. Past Progressive (Questions)

Directions Part I: Answer the following questions in the positive form. Some of the questions are past tense and some of the questions are past progressive tense.

Example: Was Elizabeth reading a bedtime story to her son when he fell asleep?
            Yes, she was reading a bedtime story to her son when he fell asleep.

1.   Was Marcia shopping when her new car was stolen?

2.   Was Dana asleep when you arrived?

3.   Were they eating dinner when the telephone rang?

4.   Did you try Janeth's spinach empanadas?

5.   Was Josefa fired from the store?

6.   Was your baby taking a nap when the salesman knocked at the door?

7.   Was Debbie cooking dinner when the fire started?

8.   Were Flora and Cynthia absent last Friday?

9.   Was Gabriela driving when the accident happened?

10.   Did Andrew break his arm at work?

Directions Part II: Answer the questions in the negative form.

Example: Was Elizabeth reading a bedtime story to her son when he fell asleep?
            No, she wasn't reading a bedtime story to her son when he fell asleep.

Future Progressive Verb Tense

The future progressive expresses that an action will be in progress at a time in the future.

I will be doing   We will be doing
He will be doing   You will be doing
She will be doing   They will be doing
It will be doing

Example: He <u>will be working</u> at ten this evening.

In a time clause, the verb is present tense, but the meaning is future.

Example: Tara will be working in the garden <u>when Michelle arrives</u>.

> Directions: Use the future progressive <u>or</u> the present tense.

1.   I _____ (wash) my car when you arrive.

2.   When Frank comes, his wife _____ (wait) for him.

3.   Gina _____ (cook) dinner while Eric takes a shower.

4.   While Lee _____ (be) at school, Fran will be making a cake.

5.   Paul _____ (drive) the car while his wife sleeps in the backseat.

6.   Bob _____ (relax) on a beach in Hawaii tomorrow.

7.   Marla _____ (come) soon.

8.   When I turn sixty, I _____ (enjoy) retirement.

9.   Next week, Janet _____ (visit) her aunt in Miami.

10.   Don't start the dishwasher now! Andrea _____ (take) a nap in about fifteen minutes.

Future Progressive (Negative Form)

I will not / won't be working
He will not / won't be working
She will not / won't be working
It will not / won't be working

You will not / won't be working
We will not / won't be working
They will not / won't be working

The future progressive verb tense is used to show that two actions will happen at the same time in the future.

Directions: Change the following sentences to the negative form.

1. Roger <u>will be studying</u> at the library tomorrow night.

2. When his wife calls, Emilio <u>will be working</u>.

3. Glenn <u>will be living</u> in Japan at this time next year.

4. You <u>will be talking</u> after the test begins.

5. Fred <u>will be playing</u> in the yard when his mother comes home.

6. Sue <u>will be swimming</u> in the pool later this afternoon.

7. Bert <u>will be waiting</u> in his car when you get out of school.

8. Maricela <u>will be visiting</u> her relatives in Argentina this summer.

9. When his children get home, Viper <u>will be working</u> on his motorcycle.

10. Pam <u>will be watching</u> a movie when her mother comes home.

Future Progressive (Questions)

Will I be talking?   Will you be talking?
Will he be talking?   Will we be talking?
Will she be talking?   Will they be talking?
Will it be talking?

Directions: Change the following sentences to questions.

1.   Sharon will be doing her homework later tonight.

2.   Theodore and Sandy will be getting off the school bus at two o'clock.

3.   When the war starts, Dale will be living in Mexico.

4.   Sophia will be eating her lunch when the boss comes.

5.   Dr. McGregor will be talking to Joseph about his heart attack.

6.   Steven will be learning Japanese while he is living in Tokyo.

7.   Roberta will be preparing snacks when her guests arrive.

8.   Hilda will be traveling in Greece on July 4th.

9.   Bob and Brent will be playing tennis while Mindy is studying.

10. The police will be writing tickets for school zone speeders tomorrow morning.

Progressive Tenses (Positive, Negative, and Question Forms)

Present Progressive
Positive Form: He is working in a restaurant.
Negative Form: He is not/isn't working in a restaurant.
Question Form: Is he working in a restaurant?

Past Progressive
Positive Form: He was working in a restaurant.
Negative Form: He was not/wasn't working in a restaurant.
Question Form: Was he working in a restaurant?

Future Progressive
Positive Form: He will be working in a restaurant.
Negative Form: He will not/won't be working in a restaurant.
Question Form: Will he be working in a restaurant?

Directions Part I: Change the following sentences to negative form.
Directions Part II: Change the following sentences to question form.

---

1.   Janeth is driving a green car.

2.   Angelica was cooking dinner when the doorbell rang.

3.   Dolores and Cynthia are visiting relatives in Mexico.

4.   Jose was wearing blue jeans on Friday.

5.   Sandra and Karen will be taking a GED test next month.

6.   Catalina will be taking her GED test in February.

7.   Maria is eating a cookie right now.

8.   They were living in California last year.

9.   I am telling a joke to Juanita.

10.   The class will be meeting on Saturday morning.

Present, Future, or Future Progressive

Time clauses begin with words such as <u>when</u>, <u>before</u>, <u>after</u>, <u>as soon as</u>, <u>until</u>, <u>while</u> and include a subject and a verb. <u>While</u> shows that two actions happen simultaneously. <u>Before</u>, <u>after</u>, <u>as soon as</u>, <u>until</u>, and <u>when</u> emphasize the completion of one action before the other action occurs.

Examples: Jessica <u>will be shopping</u> **while** Anita <u>is cleaning</u> the house.
              Gary <u>is going to go</u> to bed **after** he <u>finishes</u> his homework.

Directions: Use the present, future, <u>or</u> future progressive verb tense.

1. After the rain _____ (stop), I am going to wash my car.

2. There will be relief when the war _____ (be) over.

3. Pete _____ (finish) his work before he leaves.

4. As soon as Ed finishes lunch, he _____ (take) a nap.

5. When it stops raining, I _____ (walk) to the store to get some milk.

6. When you get home, the baby _____ (sleep).

7. David _____ (drive) me to work later.

8. Dean _____ (go) to college next August.

9. Until you _____ (admit) your mistakes, you won't make any progress in your therapy.

10. Manuel _____ (travel) to Tijuana next month.

44

Progressive Tense Review

Directions: Complete each of the following sentences by using the present progressive, past progressive, or future progressive.

1. Yolanda _____ (drink) apple juice.

2. Sergio and Victor _____ (talk) when the test began.

3. The class _____ (test) next Friday.

4. Pablo _____ (take) a GED class in Galena Park when he found a job.

5. Joe was washing his car while Sally _____ (shop) for groceries.

6. Raul _____ (visit) his sick friend in the hospital tomorrow.

7. Look! Carlos _____ (kiss) Lucinda.

8. Lou _____ (spend) his birthday in Italy next year.

9. Please be quiet! I _____ (try) to listen to the news.

10. Dora _____ (soak) in the bathtub when Alexandra finished her homework.

Progressive Verb Tense Review

Directions: Correct the mistakes in the following sentences.

1.   Dolores wo'nt be working when Cynthia goes to college next September.

2.   Will be Guadalupe taking GED classes next fall?

3.   Was Esperanza cook dinner when her son got home?

4.   Were Felix and Martha studying grammar right now?

5.   Karen will be going to college after she will receive her GED.

6.   Were Sharon and Roman argueing when the police came?

7.   When the teacher walked into the room Patricia was talking to Bertha.

8.   Sandra was wearing a white shirt tomorrow.

9.   Oralia selling jewelry as a part-time job.

10. Who will teaching the class next week?

Simple and Progressive Verb Tense Review

Directions Part I: Answer the following questions in the positive form.

Example: Does Terry work in an office?   Yes, she works in an office.

1.   Do you have four children?

2.   Were you living in Galveston when the hurricane hit?

3.   Is Felix wearing a purple shirt?

4.   Are you going to attend the GED class next fall?

5.   Was Angela upset by her son's poor grades?

6.   Will Arturo be attending the ESL class at this time next year?

7.   Does Bertha like her new house?

8.   Is the baby's diaper dirty?

9.   Did Maricela study for the test?

10.   Does Janeth like sushi?

Directions Part II: Answer the questions in the negative form.

Example: Does Terry work in an office?
           No, she doesn't work in an office.

Present Perfect Verb Tense

Use the present perfect tense to show that an action happened in the past with no specific mention of time. When something happened is not important, just that it happened.

Examples: Linda <u>has washed</u> her hands.
They <u>have finished</u> their homework.

<u>For</u> and <u>since</u> are used to show length of time and duration.

Examples: Jose has taught Spanish <u>for eleven years</u>.
Jose has taught Spanish <u>since 1999</u>.

If, when something happened is important, then use the past tense.

Example: Joe <u>bought</u> his house in 1997.

I have worked
You have worked
We have worked
They have worked

He has worked
She has worked
It has worked

Directions: Use the present perfect verb tense in the blanks.

1.   I am not hungry. I _____ already _____ (eat) dinner.

2.   Chris _____ (finish) his test.

3.   We _____ (live) in Pasadena since 1997.

4.   Eddie and Leticia _____ (be) married for eleven years.

5.   Fidel _____ finally _____ (do) his work.

6.   Cindy _____ (work) at this company for nine months.

7.   We _____ (see) that movie many times.

8.   She _____ already _____. (leave)

9.   John _____ (pay) the bill.

10.   Dave _____ (study) Spanish before.

Present Perfect (#2)

Use have or has with the past participle verb form to make the present perfect verb tense.

Examples: I <u>have taught</u> English since 1988.
He <u>has had</u> a headache for more than an hour.

The purpose of <u>for</u> and <u>since</u> with the present perfect tense is to describe an action that began in the past and continues to the present.

Examples: Juana has owned that car <u>for three years</u>.
Juana has owned that car <u>since 2008</u>.
(Juana still owns that car.)

However, <u>for</u> can also be used with the past tense to show that an action began and ended in the past.

Example: I <u>taught</u> English for twenty years. (I no longer teach English. The action is in the past tense.)

Directions: Use the present perfect verb tense to complete each sentence.

1.   Doug _____ (teach) math since 1991.

2.   Cathy _____ (drive) this car for ten years.

3.   We _____ (dine) at that restaurant several times.

4.   They _____ (be) divorced since 2006.

5.   Carl _____ (have) a cold for a week.

6.   The students _____ (complete) the exam.

7.   The class _____. (begin)

8.   Bill _____ (come) from Colorado.

9.   The pen _____ (run) out of ink.

10. She _____ (watch) this soap opera for many years.

49

Past vs. Present Perfect

Use the past tense with a specific mention of time. If something happened in the past, but there is no specific mention of time, use the present perfect.

Remember that <u>since</u> and <u>for</u> are used with the present perfect to express duration and length of time. <u>Since</u> cannot be used with the past tense, but <u>for</u> can be used with the past tense to show that an action began and ended in the past.

Directions: Use the past or present perfect tense of the verb in parentheses. If there is a specific mention of time, use the past tense. If there is no specific mention of time, use the present perfect.

1. Diane _____ (write) a letter to her parents last week.

2. I _____ (hear) that song many times.

3. Jeff _____ (borrow) some money from me last month.

4. The Great Depression _____ (begin) in 1929.

5. Anthony _____ (be) sick for the last two days.

6. Tom and Tammy _____ (have) many problems in their marriage.

7. Maria _____ (bring) the papers to my office a few minutes ago.

8. He _____ (live) in London for twelve years.

9. Blake _____ (work) for this company since 2001.

10. Elizabeth _____ (take) a sick day yesterday.

Present Perfect (Negative Form)

I have not / haven't eaten
You have not / haven't eaten
We have not / haven't eaten
They have not / haven't eaten

He has not / hasn't eaten
She has not / hasn't eaten
It has not / hasn't eaten

If something began in the past and continues to the present, then use the present perfect verb tense. Use <u>since</u> to show that an action began in the past and continues to the present.

Example: I have followed his advice <u>since</u> 2006.

Directions: Change these sentences from positive to negative.

1.   Mickey has started his acting career.

2.   Orlando and Olivia have been to Canada three times.

3.   We have learned many things since this class began.

4.   Cynthia has completed her research paper.

5.   Daniel has read that book many times.

6.   I have thought about my problems for a long time.

7.   The engine has stopped.

8.   You have broken my stereo.

9.   The weather has been cold for several days.

10.   Joe has found his laptop computer.

Present Perfect (Questions)

Have I gone?   Has he gone?

Have you gone?   Has she gone?

Have we gone?   Has it gone?

Have they gone?

Use the present perfect tense when an action happened (or not) in the past with no mention of a specific time.

Example: Has Gage <u>ever</u> played tennis?

Gage is twenty four years old. Has he played tennis one time during his twenty four years? It doesn't matter if he liked it or was any good at it, but that he played tennis once to this point in his young life.

Directions: Use the correct form of the present perfect to make a question.

1.   _____ Frank _____ (go) to the doctor yet?

2.   _____ they _____ (sell) their house?

3.   How long _____ Bob _____ (have) a beard?

4.   _____ you _____ (pay) your taxes yet?

5.   When _____ she ever _____ (be) nice to me?

6.   Why _____ we _____ (tolerate) Lucia's behavior for so long?

7.   _____ you ever _____ (be) to Italy?

8.   What _____ they _____ (learn) in Kindergarten?

9.   How long _____ you _____ (live) in Houston?

10.   _____ Allan _____ (finish) his assignment?

Present Perfect vs. Past (Questions)

Directions Part I: Answer the following questions in the positive (affirmative) form. Some of the questions are present perfect, and some of the questions are past tense.

Examples: Has Lisa gone to bed yet? (Present Perfect)
Yes, she has gone to bed.

Did you enjoy the party last night? (Past)
Yes, I enjoyed the party last night.

1. Has Jose found a job?

2. Did Dorothy go to Corpus Christi last week?

3. Was Sandy sick yesterday?

4. Has Frank seen the doctor about his headaches?

5. Were they happy in their old neighborhood?

6. Did Lucy go to college?

7. Has Esperanza finished her essay?

8. Did Linda lose a library book last month?

9. Have you spoken to your supervisor about her rude comments?

10. Was Magda a good student?

Directions Part II: Answer the questions in the negative form.

Examples: Has Lisa gone to bed yet? (Present Perfect)
No, she hasn't gone to bed yet.

Did you enjoy the party last night? (Past)
No, I didn't enjoy the party last night.

Past Perfect Verb Tense (Rules)

Positive (Affirmative) Form

I had worked

You had worked

He had worked

We had worked

She had worked

They had worked

It had worked

Negative Form

I had not / hadn't worked

You had not / hadn't worked

He had not / hadn't worked

We had not / hadn't worked

She had not / hadn't worked

They had not / hadn't worked

It had not / hadn't worked

Question Form

Had I worked?

Had you worked?

Had he worked?

Had we worked?

Had she worked?

Had they worked?

Had it worked?

The past perfect tense is used with the past tense to show that the action in the past perfect began and ended before the past tense action happened.

Example: Marisa <u>had made</u> dinner by the time John <u>came</u> home.

Marisa made dinner first. Then John came home.

Marisa had dinner ready and waiting and then at some time later, John came home. Both actions happened in the past.

<u>By the time John came home</u> *is a time clause. A time clause is a dependent clause that has a subject and a verb.*

Past Perfect

Directions: Use the past perfect verb tense in the blank.

Example: Joanne *had run* five laps around the indoor track before Jose
arrived at the gym. (before Jose arrived at the gym = time
clause)
First, Joanne ran five laps around the indoor track.
Then, Jose arrived at the gym.

1. Kelvin _____ (do) his homework before his father
   came home.

2. Gary _____ (finish) dinner when his children got
   home from the movies.

3. By the time the bus stopped at his house, Ralph _____
   (eat) breakfast.

4. The sun _____ (set) before George and Doug got
   home from their fishing trip.

5. Before her mother returned from the mall, Gracie _____
   (clean) the kitchen.

6. Chayo _____ (milk) the cows when her husband got to
   the ranch.

7. Martina _____ (complete) the paperwork by the
   time the nurse called her into the examination room.

8. After Catalina _____ (take) a shower, she drank a
   cup of hot tea.

9. The teacher began his lecture after the students _____
   (stop) talking.

10. Angelica _____ (leave) the park before it started to
    rain.

Past Perfect (Negative Form)

Directions: Put the negative form of the past perfect in the blank.

Example: By the time we *finished* the grammar exercise, the teacher had not/hadn't returned from the office.

1.   Sandra _____ (eat) lunch before her GED class began.

2.   It _____ (stop) raining when our ESL class was over.

3.   I _____ (see) any of his paintings before I visited the art museum.

4.   Until I met Theresa at a Japanese restaurant last night, I _____ (see) her in many years.

5.   Gregoria _____ (leave) the party when her former boyfriend arrived.

6.   When Anna got home, her son _____ (do) his math homework.

7.   Peter _____ (start) the yard work when his dad came home.

8.   I am glad Joe _____ (buy) a new car before he lost his job.

9.   Our car _____ (run) out of gas by the time we reached the station.

10.   The class _____ (study) algebra before they began geometry.

Past Perfect (Questions)

Directions: Put the correct question form in the blanks. The questions are past, present perfect, or past perfect tense.

Examples: <u>Did</u> Sandra <u>start</u> a new job last week? (time)
<u>Has</u> Sandra <u>started</u> a new job? (no specific time)
<u>Had</u> Sandra <u>started</u> a new job before she *won* the lottery?

1. _____ the teacher ever _____ (be) to Puerto Rico?

2. _____ Emily _____ (visit) Japan before she took the trip to Tokyo last year?

3. What _____ Felix _____ (eat) before he got food poisoning?

4. When _____ Felix _____ (get) food poisoning?

5. I have been so worried about you! Where _____ you _____ (be)?

6. Adrianna is a very good student. How long _____ she _____ (study) English?

7. _____ Bill _____ (become) a millionaire before he turned thirty?

8. _____ the children _____ (learn) English by the time they came to the United States?

9. _____ Martha and her son _____ (enjoy) the concert last Saturday?

10. I was absent the last three days. I missed the lessons about the past perfect tense. _____ (be) the grammar exercises easy?

Future Perfect Verb Tense

Positive (Affirmative) Form

I will have eaten

He will have eaten

She will have eaten

It will have eaten

You will have eaten

We will have eaten

They will have eaten

Negative Form

I will not / won't have eaten

He will not / won't have eaten

She will not / won't have eaten

It will not / won't have eaten

You will not / won't have eaten

We will not / won't have eaten

They will not / won't have eaten

Question Form

Will I have eaten?

Will he have eaten?

Will she have eaten?

Will it have eaten?

Will you have eaten?

Will we have eaten?

Will they have eaten?

Use the future perfect in combination with a time clause to show that the future perfect action will begin and end first before the other action will happen.

Example: George <u>will have finished</u> his homework by the time his father gets home from work.

First, George will finish his homework. Second, his father will get home from work. <u>By the time his father gets home from work</u> is a time clause.

Future Perfect Verb Tense

Directions: Supply the future perfect tense <u>or</u> present tense in the blanks. Remember to use the present tense in a time clause.

Example: Mark <u>will have taken</u> a bath ***before his parents get home from dinner.*** (will have taken = future perfect) (before his parents get home from dinner = time clause)

1.   By the time I _____ (see) you in July, I will have graduated from college.

2.   Guillermina _____ (finish) her homework by the time she goes to the movie tonight.

3.   On September 1st, Michael _____ (teach) at this school for seven years.

4.   Eric will have showered and shaved by the time his wife _____ (wake) up.

5.   When we get to the airport tomorrow afternoon, Jim's plane _____ (arrive).

6.   At this rate, Andres _____ (have) five wives by the time he dies.

7.   Harry _____ (pay) for lunch before Jose returns from the bathroom.

8.   Tim will have practiced before his match _____ (begin).

9.   Monday, Rick _____ (drive) for eleven hours by the time he reaches Houston.

10.   Paulo _____ (take) his medicine before he goes to bed.

Future Perfect (Negative Form)

Examples: Juanita is going to visit Canada next week. (Future)
Juanita is not/isn't going to visit Canada next week.

Joe will have washed the car before Maria cuts the grass.
Joe will not/won't have washed the car before Maria cuts the grass. (Future Perfect)

1.   It is going to rain tomorrow.

2.   The teachers are going to have a meeting next week.

3.   Robert will be studying geometry when his sister gets home.

4.   Lisa will have finished her errands before her children get out of school.

5.   Mark will have left the office by the time Marta gets back.

6.   Ruby will help you.

7.   Kay will have submitted her resignation before the new boss starts next month.

8.   Dave is going to receive the check next Friday.

9.   The GED students will have studied fractions before they begin algebra.

10. Glenn's team is going to win the next game.

Future Perfect (Questions)

Directions Part I: Answer the following questions in the affirmative form. Some of the questions are future, future progressive, or future perfect.

Example: Is Sandra going to start a new job next month? (Future)
Yes, she is going to start a new job next month.

1.   Will the weather be cold tomorrow?

2.   Will Candy have saved enough money for a down payment by the time her husband returns from Iraq?

3.   Are you going to have a conference with your son's teacher next Monday?

4.   Will you close the door?

5.   Will Luis have completed his report by six o'clock?

6.   Will Carmen have had breakfast before she goes to the doctor?

7.   Will the children be playing in the driveway while their father fixes the garage door?

8.   Is Nidia going to work next Sunday?

9.   Will the students have received their certification before the teacher retires next year?

10.   Will you answer the phone?

Directions Part II: Answer the questions in the negative form.

Example: Will you be attending Easter service on April 12th? (Future Progressive)
No, I will not be attending Easter service on April 12th.

Present Perfect Progressive Verb Tense

<u>Positive (Affirmative) Form</u>

I have been working

You have been working

We have been working

They have been working

He has been working

She has been working

It has been working

<u>Negative Form</u>

I have not / haven't been working

You have not / haven't been working

We have not / haven't been working

They have not / haven't been working

He has not / hasn't been working

She has not / hasn't been working

It has not / hasn't been working

<u>Question Form</u>

Have I been working?

Have you been working?

Have we been working?

Have they been working?

Has he been working?

Has she been working?

Has it been working?

The present perfect progressive emphasizes the duration of an action that began in the past and continues to the present.

Example: Chris <u>has been teaching</u> at the college ***since 1999***.

The present perfect progressive and the present perfect have the same meaning when an action began in the past and continues to the present.

Example: Chris <u>has taught</u> at the college ***since 1999***.

Do not use the "to be" verb as the progressive verb in the present perfect progressive verb tense.

Example: I <u>have been being</u> sick for the last few days. (Incorrect)
          I <u>have been</u> sick for the last few days. (Correct/Present Perfect)

Present Perfect to Present Perfect Progressive

Example: Sue <u>has taken</u> Spanish for the last two semesters.
　　　　　 Sue <u>has been taking</u> Spanish for the last two semesters.

1.   Flora <u>has eaten</u> jalapeños for ten minutes.

2.   Patricia <u>has studied</u> English since 2007.

3.   Soledad <u>has lived</u> in Houston for nine years.

4.   I <u>have played</u> tennis for several years.

5.   The students <u>have practiced</u> their speeches since May.

6.   Maria <u>has taken</u> steroid injections since last summer.

7.   Oralia <u>has worked</u> with Dr. Smith for eight years.

8.   Linda <u>has sat</u> quietly in that chair for five minutes.

9.   Sheila <u>has slept</u> for over twelve hours.

10.   You <u>have argued</u> with him for fifteen minutes.

Present Perfect Progressive vs. Present Perfect

Stative verbs are non-progressive. The present perfect is used with stative verbs to describe an action that began in the past and continues to the present.

Example: Peter <u>has envied</u> John all his life. (envy is a stative verb)

When the present perfect progressive is used without any specific mention of time, it shows an action in progress recently.

Example: He <u>has been living</u> in a hotel.

Directions: Fill in the blank with the present perfect progressive tense <u>or</u> the present perfect tense.

---

1.   Javier _____ (play) soccer for two hours.

2.   Hector _____ (know) Elise for many years.

3.   Betty and Charlie _____ (work) at the hospital since 2004.

4.   Alma _____ (be) to Los Angeles several times.

5.   We _____ (live) in Dallas since 1987.

6.   Lola _____ (sleep) on the sofa many times.

7.   It _____ (rain) all morning.

8.   The students _____ (use) this grammar book.

9.   They _____ (do) very little work lately.

10. Lenny _____ (take) drugs since he was fifteen.

Present Perfect Progressive (Negative Form)

Directions: Change the following sentences to negative form. The sentences are present, present progressive, present perfect, or present perfect progressive.

Examples: Jackie <u>has</u> three children. (Present Tense/Positive)
Jackie <u>doesn't have</u> three children. (Present Tense/Negative)
Nancy <u>has left</u> her office. (Present Perfect Tense/Positive)
Nancy <u>hasn't left</u> her office. (Present Perfect Tense/Negative)

1. Guadalupe <u>is</u> absent today.

2. Emilio <u>has been studying</u> English for five years.

3. Maria <u>drives</u> a red car.

4. Bertha <u>has worked</u> in a restaurant.

5. Mario <u>is drinking</u> a cup of tea.

6. Hayde's wine club <u>meets</u> every Saturday afternoon.

7. Cristela and Laura <u>are wearing</u> blue jeans.

8. They <u>have been waiting</u> since six o'clock.

9. Alma and Leidy <u>are</u> angry with their teacher.

10. I <u>have been</u> to Mexico City many times.

Present Perfect Progressive

Directions: Answer the following questions in complete sentences.

Examples: How long has May been talking on the phone? (an hour)
She has been talking on the phone for an hour.

How long has May been talking on the phone? (1:30)
She has been talking on the phone since 1:30.

1. How long has Mario been working at the hospital? (five years)

2. How long has Mario been working at the hospital? (2004)

3. How long have you been playing golf? (twenty years)

4. How long have you been playing golf? (1989)

5. How long has Bertha been living in Texas? (four years)

6. How long has Bertha been living in Texas? (2005)

7. How long have they been studying Japanese? (six months)

8. How long have they been studying Japanese? (November)

9. How long have the dogs been barking? (one hour)

10. How long have the dogs been barking? (6:30)

Past Perfect Progressive Verb Tense

Positive (Affirmative) Form

I had been waiting
You had been waiting
We had been waiting
They had been waiting

He had been waiting
She had been waiting
It had been waiting

Negative Form

I had not/hadn't been waiting
You had not/hadn't been waiting
We had not/hadn't been waiting
They had not/hadn't been waiting

He had not/hadn't been waiting
She had not/hadn't been waiting
It had not/hadn't been waiting

Question Form

Had I been waiting?
Had you been waiting?
Had we been waiting?
Had they been waiting?

Had he been waiting?
Had she been waiting?
Had it been waiting?

The past perfect progressive verb tense emphasizes the duration of an activity that was in progress before another activity or time in the past.

Example: Andrea <u>had been driving</u> for twelve hours by the time she <u>reached</u> Miami.

The past perfect progressive verb tense also shows an action in progress close in time to another action or activity in the past.

Example: Luisa's fingers <u>were</u> tired because she <u>had been typing</u> on the computer for thirty minutes.

Past Perfect Progressive

Use the past perfect progressive to show the duration of an action that was in progress before another action or time in the past.

Example: The phone <u>had been ringing</u> for thirty seconds before Joe answered it.

Directions: Fill in the blank with the past perfect progressive.

1.   Mike _____ (feel) ill for three days before he finally went to the doctor.

2.   Erica arrived at seven o'clock. I _____ (wait) for her since five-thirty.

3.   Sean _____ (work) at the radio station for nine years when he got fired.

4.   Lou _____ (surf) the Internet for two hours before he got bored.

5.   Charles couldn't answer the teacher's question because he _____ (daydream) for five minutes.

6.   The couple _____ (fight) for twenty minutes before the police arrived.

7.   Gene _____ (run) for sixteen minutes before he became tired.

8.   Phil _____ (play) tennis for three years before he won a match against his big brother.

9.   I _____ (watch) the movie for ninety minutes when the electricity went out.

10.   Fabian _____ (study) English for two years before he was able to carry on a conversation with his neighbor.

Past Perfect Progressive (Negative Form)

The past perfect progressive verb tense emphasizes the duration of an action that was in progress before another action or time in the past.

Example: Marisol <u>had been living</u> in Spain for five months when she met Raul.

Marisol <u>had not/hadn't been living</u> in Spain for five months when she met Raul. (Marisol met Raul after three or four months of living in Spain, but not five months.)

Directions: Change the following sentences to the negative form. The sentences are past, past progressive, past perfect, <u>or</u> past perfect progressive.

1.   Chuck <u>went</u> to the dentist yesterday.

2.   Terry <u>had left</u> the room when Chris entered.

3.   Cindy <u>was crying</u> at the end of the movie.

4.   I <u>played</u> baseball in high school.

5.   Anthony and Duane <u>had been wrestling</u> for a few minutes when Duane broke his leg.

6.   Alma <u>was doing</u> her math homework when her mother got home from the grocery store.

7.   Lisa and Larry <u>were</u> sick last night.

8.   Gina <u>took</u> sociology in college.

9.   Maria <u>had eaten</u> lunch when I called.

10.   The mother <u>put</u> baby powder on her son's diaper rash.

Past Perfect Progressive – Questions

Directions: The following questions are past, past progressive, past perfect, or past perfect progressive. The answers are in parentheses. The questions are information or yes/no questions. Please answer the questions in complete sentences.

Examples: Did you return the book to the library last night? (no)
No, I didn't return the book to the library last night. (Past)

What did you do last night? (eat dinner, watch television, and answer e-mails)
I ate dinner, watched television, and answered e-mails. (Past)

1. What color was Guadalupe's dress? (pink)

2. Did Emilio attend class yesterday? (no)

3. What was Wanda doing when you called? (scrub the toilet)

4. When was your daughter's birthday party? (last Saturday)

5. How long had the engine been running before the car ran out of gas? (for one hour)

6. How was the weather in Boston? (cold and rainy)

7. What was Esperanza wearing yesterday? (pink pants and a black sweater)

8. Had the repairman fixed your refrigerator by the time you left for Florida? (yes)

9. What did your family have for dinner last night? (chicken fried steak, mashed potatoes, and green beans)

10. Had Margarita made breakfast by the time Rafael woke up? (no)

Past Perfect Progressive - Review

Directions: Correct the mistakes in the sentences. The sentences are past, past progressive, past perfect, or past perfect progressive. The mistakes have been underlined to help you.

Example: Maria was making dinner _after_ her husband was taking a shower. (Incorrect)

Maria was making dinner _while_ her husband was taking a shower. (Correct/Two actions are taking place at the same time in the past.)

1. Did Mike **_took_** his vacation last month?

2. I was **_swiming_** when it started to rain.

3. He had eaten the ham sandwich **_after_** he ate his dessert.

4. Felix **_had dating_** Martha for six years before they became husband and wife.

5. Dave **_was felt_** sick yesterday.

6. Manuel and Mario **_was_** painting the garage door when Mario's wife came home.

7. Beatriz had **_wrote_** her essay before she went to class.

8. Had **_been the couple_** fighting for twenty minutes by the time the police arrived?

9. I was cutting the grass in the front yard while my daughter **_rides_** her bicycle.

10. Olivia had **_came_** home before the storm began.

Future Perfect Progressive Verb Tense

<u>Positive (Affirmative) Form</u>

I will have been listening	He will have been listening
You will have been listening	She will have been listening
We will have been listening	It will have been listening
They will have been listening	

The future perfect progressive verb tense emphasizes the duration of an action that was in progress before another activity or time in the future.

Example: Andrea **will have been driving** for twelve hours by the time she reaches Miami. (<u>by the time she **reaches** Miami</u> is a time clause. The verb is in the present tense, but the meaning is future.)

Directions: Use the future perfect progressive tense in the blanks.

1.   Gerald _____ (work) for three hours by the time he finishes his report.

2.   By the time I get home, Lisa _____ (sleep) for an hour.

3.   Dana _____ (live) in Hawaii for six weeks before her house is ready.

4.   Ted _____ (study) for several months by the time he takes his law school entrance exam.

5.   Lily and Martha _____ (do) their homework for two hours before they stop.

6.   Before we take a break, we _____ (drive) for three hours.

7.   Tom _____ (practice) for a year before he is ready to play golf.

8.   Before she feels better, Paula _____ (take) therapy for a few weeks.

9.   Jim _____ (weed) for an hour before he adds mulch to the garden.

10.   They _____ (nap) for thirty minutes before their mother gets home.

Future Perfect vs. Future Perfect Progressive

The <u>future perfect</u> is used to express that an action will be completed before another time or event in the future. The <u>future perfect progressive</u> emphasizes the duration of an action that will be in progress before another time or event in the future.

Examples: By the time Matthew finishes, he <u>will have read</u> thirty essays. (future perfect)
By the time Matthew finishes, he <u>will have been reading</u> essays for three hours. (future perfect progressive)

Directions: Use the future perfect <u>or</u> the future perfect progressive.

---

1. Fred _____ (eat) lunch by the time we leave.

2. Max _____ (save) for two years before he has enough money for a car.

3. Snake _____ (repair) the motorcycle for an hour before he completes the job.

4. The first baseball game _____ (finish) before the second baseball game begins.

5. Next May, I _____ (teach) math for six years.

6. Victor _____ (clean) his storage shed for several hours before it is empty.

7. On May 1st, I _____ (be) on the avocado diet for six weeks.

8. When Natasha returns from maternity leave, her secretary _____ (do) all her reports.

9. It is 9:30. By 11:30, I _____ (wait) for two hours.

10. Julio _____ (drink) four cups of coffee by the time his wife is ready to go.

Future Perfect Progressive (Negative and Question Forms)

The future perfect progressive verb tense emphasizes the duration of an action that was in progress before another activity or time in the future.

Negative Form

I will not/won't have been speaking

You will not/won't have been speaking

He will not/won't have been speaking

She will not/won't have been speaking

It will not/won't have been speaking

We will not/won't have been speaking

They will not/won't have been speaking

Question Form

Will I have been speaking?

Will you have been speaking?

Will he have been speaking?

Will she have been speaking?

Will it have been speaking?

Will we have been speaking?

Will they have been speaking?

Future Perfect Progressive – Review

Directions: Correct the mistakes in the following sentences. The sentences are future, future progressive, future perfect, or future perfect progressive. The mistakes have been underlined to make it easier.

Example: Marcos will be sleeping when you **will** come. (Incorrect)
Marcos will be sleeping when you come. (Correct)

1. Lupe **will** go to Mexico City next month.

2. By the time she retires next year, Professor Martinez **has been teaching** for twenty years.

3. Felix and Emilio **is** going to take a break in ten minutes.

4. On Friday, my brother will be working while his family **are** visiting San Antonio.

5. You will have **began** your chores by the time Andrew wakes up.

6. Will **have David** been living in his house for fifteen years before he needs a new roof?

7. Dawn will have bought her dream house before she **will be** fifty years old.

8. Is the class going to finish **last** Friday?

9. Catalina will be attending college **after** she is working a fulltime job.

10. They **wo'nt** have sent the payment by the time they get an overdue notice.

Verb Tense Review

Directions: Supply the correct verb tense in the following sentences.

Example: Pat _____ (ride) her bike to school every Friday.

Pat <u>rides</u> her bike to school every Friday. (Present)

1.   Daniel _____ (sit) in the principal's office right now.

2.   We _____ (study) Chapter Two last week.

3.   My children _____ (see) that movie many times.

4.   I like my job. I _____ (work) as a laboratory technician for the last seven years.

5.   Vickie _____ (sleep) when you come home from the store.

6.   The employees were leaving when the manager and assistant manager _____ (arrive).

7.   Alma _____ (fly) to Costa Rica tomorrow morning.

8.   Bernard _____ (swim) twenty laps in the pool three days a week.

9.   Last week's grammar lessons _____ (be) difficult.

10.   Kris _____ already _____ (leave) when Roxanne called the office.

Part II

Verb Usage

Pages 78 – 145

Spelling Rules for Past Tense Regular Verbs

Regular verbs in the past tense end in ed. Regular verbs, unlike irregular verbs, follow spelling rules for past tense conjugation.

For verbs that end in e, add d.

Example: like / liked

For one-syllable verbs that end in consonant – vowel – consonant, double the final consonant and add ed.

Example: plan / planned

For two-syllable verbs that end in consonant – vowel – consonant with pronunciation stress on the second syllable, double the final consonant and add ed.

Example: admit / admitted

An exception to the rule is never double w or x.

Examples: chew / chewed

        mix / mixed

For verbs that end in y, if the letter before the y is a vowel, add ed.

Example: pray / prayed

For verbs that end in y, if the letter before the y is a consonant, change the y to i and add ed.

Example: deny / denied

For all other regular verbs, just add ed to make the verb past tense.

Example: park / parked

Common Regular Verb Forms

For regular verbs, the simple past form and the past participle form are the same.

Examples: I <u>wash</u> my car every Saturday. (Present)
I <u>washed</u> my car last Saturday. (Past)
I <u>have</u> already <u>washed</u> my car. (Present Perfect)

1.	act	26.	decide	51.	listen
2.	add	27.	destroy	52.	live
3.	advise	28.	dry	53.	look
4.	agree	29.	end	54.	love
5.	answer	30.	enjoy	55.	miss
6.	apologize	31.	enter	56.	move
7.	argue	32.	erase	57.	need
8.	ask	33.	explain	58.	obey
9.	bake	34.	finish	59.	open
10.	beg	35.	fix	60.	own
11.	behave	36.	follow	61.	paint
12.	belong	37.	happen	62.	park
13.	borrow	38.	hate	63.	plan
14.	breathe	39.	help	64.	play
15.	brush	40.	improve	65.	pull
16.	call	41.	include	66.	push
17.	carry	42.	join	67.	reach
18.	change	43.	jump	68.	seem
19.	clean	44.	kick	69.	smile
20.	close	45.	kiss	70.	spell
21.	complain	46.	kill	71.	start
22.	cough	47.	knock	72.	stay
23.	cry	48.	laugh	73.	stop
24.	chew	49.	learn	74.	study
25.	dance	50.	like	75.	talk

Common Irregular Verb Forms – Page 1

Simple	Simple Past	Past Participle
be	was, were	been
become	became	become
begin	began	begun
bite	bit	bitten
blow	blew	blown
break	broke	broken
bring	brought	brought
build	built	built
catch	caught	caught
choose	chose	chosen
come	came	come
cut	cut	cut
do	did	done
draw	drew	drawn
drink	drank	drunk
drive	drove	driven
eat	ate	eaten
fall	fell	fallen
feed	fed	fed
feel	felt	felt
fight	fought	fought
find	found	found
fly	flew	flown
forget	forgot	forgotten
get	got	gotten / got
give	gave	given
go	went	gone
grow	grew	grown
have	had	had
hear	heard	heard
hit	hit	hit
hold	held	held
keep	kept	kept
know	knew	known

Common Irregular Verb Forms – Page 2

Simple	Simple Past	Past Participle
leave	left	left
lend	lent	lent
light	lit	lit
lose	lost	lost
make	made	made
meet	met	met
pay	paid	paid
quit	quit	quit
read	read	read
ride	rode	ridden
ring	rang	rung
run	ran	run
see	saw	seen
sell	sold	sold
send	sent	sent
set	set	set
sing	sang	sung
sink	sank	sunk
sit	sat	sat
sleep	slept	slept
speak	spoke	spoken
spend	spent	spent
stand	stood	stood
sweep	swept	swept
swim	swam	swum
take	took	taken
teach	taught	taught
tear	tore	torn
tell	told	told
think	thought	thought
throw	threw	thrown
understand	understood	understood
wear	wore	worn
win	won	won
write	wrote	written

Passive Voice - Rules

The active voice shows that the object receives the action of the main verb.

Example: Erica delivers the mail to our office.
                 Erica = subject
                 delivers = verb
                 the mail = object

The passive voice shows that the subject is receiving the action of the verb.

Example: The mail is delivered by Erica to our office.
                 The mail = subject
                 is = present tense form of the "to be" verb
                 delivered = past participle form of deliver
                 by Erica = prepositional phrase

The meaning of both examples is exactly the same.

Form the passive voice by using the appropriate form of "to be" and the past participle form of the main verb.

Active Voice
Present – Sue returns the movie.
Present Progressive – Sue is returning the movie.
Present Perfect – Sue has returned the movie.
Past – Sue returned the movie.
Past Progressive – Sue was returning the movie.
Past Perfect – Sue had returned the movie.
Future (will) – Sue will return the movie.
Future (going to) – Sue is going to return the movie.
Future Perfect – Sue will have returned the movie.

The present perfect progressive, past perfect progressive, future perfect progressive, and the future progressive are rarely used in the passive voice.

Passive Voice – Rules/Page 2

Passive Voice

Present – The movie is returned by Sue.

Present Progressive – The movie is being returned by Sue

Present Perfect – The movie has been returned by Sue.

Past – The movie was returned by Sue.

Past Progressive – The movie was being returned by Sue.

Past Perfect – The movie had been returned by Sue.

Future (will) – The movie will be returned by Sue.

Future (going to) – The movie is going to be returned by Sue.

Future Perfect – The movie will have been returned by Sue.

To change an active voice sentence to passive voice, the active voice sentence must have an object (a noun following the action verb that receives the action of the verb).

Examples: Linda petted the dog. (Active)

The dog was petted by Linda. (Passive)

Linda is washing the car. (Active)

The car is being washed by Linda. (Passive)

If an active voice sentence does not have an object, the sentence cannot be changed to the passive voice.

Examples: Jay seems <u>tired</u>. (Active)

No passive voice is possible because tired is an adjective, not an object.

Passive Voice

Directions: Change the following sentences to the passive voice.

Example: Gloria <u>helped</u> my mother. (Past)
My mother <u>was helped</u> by Gloria. (was + past participle form of help)

The object in the active voice becomes the subject in the passive voice.
The subject in the active voice follows <u>by</u> in the passive voice.

1.   Fire <u>destroyed</u> my neighbor's house.

2.   Robert <u>took</u> the book from the table.

3.   Alexis <u>will eat</u> the chocolate flan.

4.   Bertha and Nora <u>have finished</u> the annual report.

5.   Mrs. Roberts <u>is going to leave</u> the tickets at the front desk.

6.   The police <u>captured</u> the purse snatcher.

7.   Many students <u>attended</u> the professor's lectures.

8.   Zoe <u>manages</u> the export division.

9.   Edward <u>returned</u> the golf clubs last night.

10.   Al <u>delivers</u> the mail every morning.

Passive Voice (More Practice)

Directions: Change the following sentences to the passive voice.

Example: Paula is typing Ana's paper. (Active)
Ana's paper is being typed by Paula. (Passive)
Ana's paper = subject
is being = to be verb/present progressive form
typed = past participle form of type
by Paula = prepositional phrase

1. Guillermo writes poetry.

2. Edgar is writing a magazine article.

3. Greg has finished Peter's homework.

4. Many people saw the car accident.

5. Security guards were protecting the armored car.

6. Doctor Ramsey has helped many children.

7. Araceli will plan the surprise party.

8. The clinic is going to offer free vaccines.

9. The frog will have eaten the spider.

10. The waitress brought my order.

Passive Voice – Even More Practice

Directions: Change the following sentences to the passive voice.

Example: Car thieves <u>are stealing</u> Bob's car. (Active)
Bob's car <u>is being</u> *stolen* by car thieves. (Passive)

Both sentences are in the present progressive verb tense. Stolen is the past participle form of the verb <u>steal</u> (stealing).

1.   A car thief <u>stole</u> Jack's car. (Past)

2.   A car thief <u>is going to steal</u> Bob's car. (Future/going to)

3.   Linda <u>ate</u> the last doughnut. (Past)

4.   Alex <u>eats</u> two pieces of toast every morning. (Present)

5.   Francisca <u>has eaten</u> raw oysters many times. (Present Perfect)

6.   Randy <u>broke</u> the cup. (Past)

7.   Vanessa <u>is going to break</u> Raquel's glasses. (Future/going to)

8.   Maria <u>is playing</u> the flute. (Present Progressive)

9.   Willie <u>has played</u> this guitar for sixteen years. (Present Perfect)

10.   Women <u>played</u> professional baseball during World War II. (Past)

Passive Voice (Negative Form)

Form negatives in the passive voice by adding <u>not</u> to the auxiliary verb.

Example: Chris <u>will not eat</u> all of the bananas. (Active)
           All of the bananas <u>will not be eaten</u> by Chris. (Passive)

Of course, the contracted form is also acceptable.

Example: Chris <u>won't eat</u> all of the bananas. (Active)
           All of the bananas <u>won't be eaten</u> by Chris. (Passive)

The active voice is more common than the passive voice. Also, even when the passive voice is possible, it may sound a bit awkward.

Directions: Change the sentences to the passive negative form.

1. Sonya doesn't write children's books.

2. Mr. White isn't writing a letter.

3. Elsy hasn't finished the invitations.

4. Cindy didn't see the fight.

5. A guard wasn't protecting the apartment complex.

6. The doctor hasn't seen many patients.

7. Freddy won't plan the party.

8. The city isn't going to fix the roads.

9. The cat won't have caught the mouse before we get home.

10. The waiter isn't filling my glass.

Passive Voice (Questions)

In a passive voice question, an auxiliary verb precedes the subject.

Example: Have the police arrested a suspect? (Active)
             Has a suspect been arrested by the police? (Passive)

The object (a suspect) becomes the subject, and the subject (the police) is used with the preposition by.

Directions: Change the questions from active voice to passive voice.

1.   Is Amy writing a letter?

2.   Did a fire destroy that house?

3.   Will Walter eat the cake?

4.   Has Bert finished the test?

5.   Had Maria done the budget when Magda returned from lunch?

6.   Is Paul cutting the grass?

7.   Are millions of people going to watch the show?

8.   Did Andrew leave the flowers?

9.   Will Lou eat the leftovers?

10.   Did Blanca find the book?

Passive to Active Voice

Directions: Change the following sentences from the passive voice to the active voice.

Example: The movie <u>was</u> <u>directed</u> by Stewart Buchanan. (Passive)
Stewart Buchanan <u>directed</u> the movie. (Active)

1.   That book was written by Pat Dawson.

2.   The building is being destroyed by fire.

3.   The city will be captured by the enemy.

4.   The magazine had been found by Nanette.

5.   The tennis rackets have been returned by Barbara.

6.   The contract will be signed by Mr. Martin.

7.   The road is going to be built by a Japanese company.

8.   Yolanda was being chased by a bear through the forest.

9.   The turkey will be cooked by Andrea tomorrow night.

10.   The tests are being graded by the teacher.

Passive Voice to Active Voice

Examples: The gift will be bought by Lance tomorrow. (Passive/Future)
Lance will buy the gift tomorrow. (Active/Future)

Has the bedroom been painted by Derek yet?
(Passive/Present Perfect)
Has Derek painted the bedroom yet? (Active/Present Perfect)

1. The bedroom is cooled by two floor fans.

2. The carpet is being vacuumed by Cindy.

3. Tonight's dinner is going to be prepared by Julia and Ingrid.

4. Have the math problems been solved by the students?

5. The tree was being trimmed by Andre when he cut his hand.

6. The trash wasn't emptied by the janitor.

7. The dirty dishes will be washed by me.

8. Have the windows been opened by Phillip?

9. The battery was replaced by Hugo.

10. Amber's toenails were painted by Marissa.

Passive Voice

In the active voice, the object receives the action of the main verb.

Example: Ross helped <u>the little girl</u>.

In the passive voice, the subject receives the action of the main verb.

Example: The little girl was <u>helped</u> by Ross.

Only transitive verbs (verbs that are followed by an object) are used in the passive.

Example: Tyra likes to sleep on the sofa. (Active)

No passive is possible because there is no object of the verb <u>sleep</u>.

Directions: Change from active voice to passive voice, if possible.

1.   My goldfish died yesterday.

2.   The program director interviewed me.

3.   Jose agrees with the president's economic policy.

4.   Farmers grow corn in Iowa.

5.   John Ayers built this house in 1932.

6.   The weather was hot on Wednesday.

7.   Did Mr. Sanchez paint the living room?

8.   The students didn't follow the teacher's instructions.

9.   Naomi is studying.

10.   Elise will have washed the dishes by the time we finish eating.

Modal Auxiliaries - Rules

An auxiliary verb is a helping verb. It comes in front of the simple form of a main verb.

The following helping verbs are called modal auxiliaries: can, could, may, might, must, should, will, would. Modal auxiliaries express a speaker's attitude and are used to convey the strength of the attitude.

Expressions that are similar to modal auxiliaries are: be able to, be going to, and have (has) to.

Auxiliary/Meaning	Example
Can/Ability	Hugo can play the guitar very well.
Could/Past Ability	I could run ten miles when I was younger.
May/Possibility	Carl may go to Spain next July.
Might/Possibility	Carl might go to Spain next July.
Must/Necessity	Every driver must have car insurance.
Should/Advisability	You should see a doctor.
Will/Future	I will drive Ed to work tomorrow.
Be Able To/Ability	I am able to juggle four balls at once.
Be Going To/Future	I am going to go to the party on Sunday.
Have (Has) To/Necessity	Arnold has to quit smoking.

Modal Auxiliaries – Can vs. Could

Can is used to show present or future ability. The negative form is cannot or can't. Could is used to show past ability. The negative form is could not or couldn't.

Examples: Elvira <u>can speak</u> Spanish fluently. (Present/Ability)

   I <u>couldn't play</u> the piano five years ago. (Past/Ability)

Directions: Fill in the blanks with the correct form of can <u>or</u> could.

1. Ruth _____ speak English very well because she has been practicing with her neighbor for several months.

2. I am sorry I _____ go to the wedding last night.

3. Raquel _____ play the guitar, but she is going to take lessons next year.

4. Five years ago, Camilo _____ drive a car however, he is a good driver now.

5. When Norma was a child, she _____ run five miles in less than thirty minutes.

6. Mickey has a beautiful home. He _____ see the Pacific Ocean from his living room window.

7. Penguins can swim, but they _____ fly.

8. _____ I borrow your car tomorrow?

9. If you are not an American citizen, you _____ vote or serve on a jury.

10. Luis _____ play basketball last night because he had a sprained ankle.

Modal Auxiliaries - May vs. Must

May is used for a polite request (with I or we) or to show possibility.

Examples: May I borrow your dictionary? (Polite Request)
He may leave the program at any time. (Possibility)

Must is used to show necessity or a strong certainty.

Examples: Lea's exam is tomorrow. She must go to class. (Necessity)
Adrianna is never absent, but she is absent today. She must be sick. (Strong Certainty)

Directions: Fill in the blank with may or must.

1. Kyle doesn't have any money. He _____ find a job soon.

2. Linda slammed the door. She _____ be angry.

3. _____ we have a party next Friday?

4. You _____ practice if you want to improve.

5. Jill is smiling from ear to ear. She _____ be happy about something.

6. Ray has had blurred vision for three weeks. He _____ go to the doctor.

7. I am not sure about my plans. I _____ take my children to the park or to the beach.

8. To get to work on time, Beverly _____ leave her house by 7:30.

9. Sean _____ quit his job to go back to school. He hasn't made a decision yet.

10. When you travel to Mexico, you _____ have a passport.

Modal Auxiliaries – Might vs. Should

Might is used to show possibility.

Example: Lupe might buy a new house. (Possibility)

Should is used for advisability.

Example: Home prices are very low right now. Lupe should buy a new house. (Advisability)

Directions: Use the correct form of might or should.

1. Joe has been sneezing for two days. He _____ have allergies.

2. _____ I invite Sean to the party?

3. Ed's company is having financial problems. In my opinion, he _____ wait to buy a new car.

4. If Ed's company continues to struggle, he _____ lose his job.

5. Leticia _____ ask her boss for a raise because she is the best employee in this company.

6. My family _____ go to New Braunfels for Memorial Day. We haven't made a decision yet.

7. Linda loves animals. She _____ become a veterinarian.

8. If I have time after work, I _____ visit my mother.

9. In my opinion, mothers _____ stay home and take care of their children.

10. There are so many good restaurants in Houston. We _____ eat Italian, Chinese, or Greek food for dinner on Saturday night.

95

Modal Auxiliaries – Will vs. Have (Has) To

Will is used for a future action.

Examples: I will help Anna with her math homework. (Willingness)
The weather will be cold and windy tomorrow. (Prediction)

Have (Has) To is used for necessity.

Example: A driver has to wear a seatbelt in Texas. (Necessity)

Directions: Use the correct form of will **or** have to.

1.   Glen's math grades are terrible! He _____ study harder if he wants to pass the class.

2.   I _____ pay the property taxes to keep my house.

3.   Patty _____ leave a tip for the waitress.

4.   There is a leak in one of our pipes. We _____ call a plumber right away.

5.   Hurricanes happen in cycles. Because of Ike, I don't think we _____ get another major hurricane for several years.

6.   Greg is unselfish, so he _____ share his food with us.

7.   Students _____ have their supplies on the first day of school.

8.   The teacher likes you very much. I am sure that he _____ write a reference letter for you.

9.   Bill's sinus condition is getting worse. He has been sick for five days. He _____ see the doctor tomorrow.

10. Marta doesn't have a car, and her house is two blocks from my house. I _____ give Martha a ride home after class.

Modal Auxiliaries - Have To vs. Must (Negative Form)

Have To in the negative form means lack of necessity.

Examples: We <u>don't have to go</u> to class next Monday because it is a holiday. (Future)
             We <u>don't have to go</u> to class today because it is a holiday. (Present)
             We <u>didn't have to go</u> to class last Monday because it was a holiday. (Past)

Must in the negative form means prohibition. There is no past tense form.

Example: You <u>must not/mustn't smoke</u> inside a hospital. (Present/Future)

Directions: Use the negative form of have to <u>or</u> must to complete the sentences.

1.   Mrs. McGee didn't give us any homework, so I _____ study
      tonight.

2.   If you encounter a lion, you _____ show fear because the lion is
      more likely to attack.

3.   Shelly _____ go to work tomorrow because it is Sunday.

4.   Mr. Jones _____ fill out a time sheet because he is the
      owner of the company.

5.   Drivers _____ drink and drive because too many innocent
      people are killed by drunk drivers every year.

6.   Julia _____ study very hard because she is a genius.

7.   You _____ insult the king. He has a temper and carries a pistol.

8.   An employee in one of my stores _____ be rude to the
      customers. I will fire a rude employee immediately.

9.   Helena _____ clean the toilet because she has a maid.

10.   My wife's birthday is next Monday. I want her to be happy. I _____ forget
      to buy some flowers for her.

Modal Auxiliaries – Be Able To vs. Be Going To

Be Able To is used to show ability.

Examples: Sid <u>is able to do</u> forty pushups in one minute. (Present)
Sid <u>was able to come</u> to the party last night. (Past)
Sid <u>will be able to attend</u> the meeting tomorrow. (Future)

Be Going To is used for future action.

Examples: Mandy and Ron <u>are going to buy</u> a vacation home. (Plan)
The Toros <u>are going to win</u> the championship. (Prediction)

Directions: Use **be able to** <u>or</u> **be going to** in the sentences.

1. My uncle _____ help me financially when I went to college.

2. Barry _____ take a trip to Corpus Christi next week.

3. Paul _____ mow the yard later today.

4. Bertha _____ stay home with her baby because her husband got a big promotion.

5. Raquel _____ type sixty words per minute.

6. The class _____ begin on July 13th.

7. Ana has found a babysitter for her son. She _____ start college next month.

8. We _____ have dinner with our friends tonight.

9. Michael and Joe _____ attend class yesterday because they weren't working.

10. Chris _____ retire early because he has saved a lot of money.

Modal Auxiliaries – Review

Directions: Complete each sentence with the proper modal auxiliary. Use each verb only one time.

be able to	have to	should
be going to	may	will
can	might	
could	must	

1. Most Americans _____ work to make a living. (Necessity)

2. Sandra _____ play three sets of tennis without getting tired when she was a teenager. (Ability)

3. Lee _____ see a podiatrist about the pain in his left foot. (Advisability)

4. Marisa _____ stay home after the baby is born. (Possibility)

5. Blanca _____ speak English well because she has been studying for two years. (Ability)

6. If I go on a strict diet and exercise regularly, I _____ lose twenty pounds in three months. (Prediction)

7. Juanita _____ attend the conference or lose her job. (Necessity)

8. Estelle _____ afford an expensive car because her husband is a well-paid executive. (Ability)

9. Dave _____ drive to Oklahoma City next weekend. (Plan)

10. _____ we join you for dinner? (Polite Request)

Modal Auxiliaries and Similar Expressions – Review

Directions: Correct the mistakes in the following sentences.

Example: Each player <u>have to have</u> his or her own set of clubs. (Incorrect)

Each player <u>has to have</u> his or her own set of clubs. (Correct)

1.   Mario <u>can be able to work</u> late tomorrow night. (Ability)

2.   It is past 11:30. I <u>must to go</u>! (Necessity)

3.   <u>May</u> she <u>borrow</u> the dictionary? (Polite Request)

4.   Patricia <u>could finish</u> the assignment tomorrow. (Ability)

5.   Matt <u>will buys</u> his first car next year. (Future/Plan)

6.   Jerry is having a heart attack. He <u>should go</u> to the emergency room. (Necessity)

7.   Lupita is never absent. She <u>might come</u> to class tomorrow. (Future/Prediction)

8.   Drivers in Texas <u>should have</u> a driver's license and liability insurance. (Necessity)

9.   This is a travel advisory for tourists. The weather in southeast Texas in July <u>may be</u> hot. (Future/Prediction)

10.   Lorena <u>was able to attend</u> school yesterday because she was very ill. (Ability)

Modal Auxiliaries – Would (Rules)

The auxiliary verb "would" has five different meanings.

Meaning	Example
Polite Request	Would you close the door?
Preference – Present/Future	I would rather drive to Austin than fly to Austin.
Preference – Past	I would rather have driven to Austin than flown to Austin.
Preference – Progressive	I would rather be playing golf than studying fractions.
Repeated Action in the Past	When I was in college, I would sleep until ten o'clock every morning.
Polite Form for Want	I would like some strawberries, please.
Unfulfilled Wish – Past	Arnold would have gone to the party, but he had to study for a final exam.

Would you as a request is considered more polite than will you.

Would is used for regularly repeated actions in the past.

Would rather expresses preference. One person, place, thing, or action is preferred more than another person, place, thing, or action.

In some situations, want can be considered too demanding. Would like is kinder and gentler compared to want.

Modal Auxiliaries – Would

Directions: Use the correct form of <u>would</u> in the blanks.

Example: When I was in high school, I _____ (go) to the
                   beach with my friends every weekend.

                   When I was in high school, I <u>would go</u> to the beach with my
                   friends every weekend. (Repeated action in the past)

1.   Helen _____ (go) to lunch with us
       yesterday, but she had a doctor's appointment.

2.   When Elvira was a child, she _____ (visit) her
       grandmother's farm every summer.

3.   The teacher _____ (eat) stuffed peppers
       wrapped with bacon than liver and onions.

4.   _____ you _____ (pass) the salt, please?

5.   The students _____ (like) to go home early.

6.   Martha _____ (study) English grammar than
       watch television.

7.   We _____ (like) some peace and quiet.

8.   The young mother _____ (take) a nap, but the
       neighbor's dog was barking.

9.   When Harry was a teenager, his family _____
       (travel) to Oklahoma every July.

10.   _____ you _____ (bring) me the
       attendance report for April?

Modal Auxiliaries – Would (More Practice)

Directions: Use the correct form of <u>would</u> to complete each sentence.

1. John _____ (dance) with his
   girlfriend than cleaning the garage.

2. David _____ (play) full court basketball two or
   three times a week when he was a young man. Now, he is
   overweight and breathes heavily when he ties his shoes.

3. Gary _____ (tell) his parents the truth,
   but he was too ashamed to admit his mistakes to them.

4. _____ you _____ (take out) the garbage,
   please?

5. Tammy _____ (like) a new vacuum
   cleaner for Mother's Day.

6. I _____ (refinish) the coffee table than buy a
   new one.

7. _____ you _____ (turn off) the air
   conditioner? It's getting cold in here.

8. No talking! I _____ (like) your undivided
   attention, please.

9. I remember the good old days of summer when children
   _____ (roam) free until it was time for dinner.
   Now, children have to be watched all the time.

10. Chris _____ (visit) Mexico last year,
    but she was scared by the news reports of violence throughout the
    country.

Modal Auxiliaries – Past Tense Form (Rules)

<u>Modal Auxiliary</u>	<u>Example</u>
Can	No past tense form
Could/Suggestion for a past action	Dave <u>could have helped</u>, but you didn't call him.
May/50% certainty	Tara didn't go to work yesterday. She <u>may have been</u> sick.
Might/50% certainty	Tara didn't go to work yesterday. She <u>might have been</u> sick.
Must/95% certainty	Tara didn't go to work yesterday. She <u>must have been</u> sick because she never misses work.
Should/Advisability	You <u>should have told</u> Dave about your money problems because he helped me when I had money problems. (You didn't tell Dave about your money problems, and now you have big problems.)
Will	No past tense form
Be Able To/Ability	We <u>were able to finish</u> our project because we worked overtime.
Be Going To/Unfulfilled Intention	I <u>was going to help</u> Michelle, but her poor attitude upset me. (My plan was to help Michelle, but I didn't help her.)
Had To/Necessity	You <u>had to turn</u> in a timesheet to get paid. (If you turned in a timesheet, you got paid.

Modal Auxiliaries – Past Tense (Easy Version)

Directions: Use the correct past tense auxiliary verb to complete each
sentence.

Example: Cristela was late yesterday. She is never late. Traffic
_____ (be) very bad. (95% Certainty)
Cristela was late yesterday. She is never late. Traffic <u>must
have been</u> very bad. (95% Certainty)

1. Sara was absent yesterday. She is absent all the time. She
_____ (be) sick or too lazy to come to school. (50%
certainty)

2. The chicken didn't smell good, but I ate it anyway. Now I have food
poisoning. I _____ (eat) it. (Advisability)

3. John _____ (watch) television, but he took his
daughters to the park instead. (Unfulfilled intention)

4. Sheila _____ (leave) early to beat traffic. (Necessity)

5. Kris _____ (help) her son with his book report. (Ability)

6. Linda _____ (study), but she fell asleep
because she was so tired. (Unfulfilled intention)

7. If Billy wanted to go on the field trip, he _____ (ask) his
parents for permission. (Suggestion)

8. Robert and Susan _____ (have) tuna fish
sandwiches for dinner, but they decided to go out to a restaurant
instead. (Unfulfilled intention)

9. The soccer team _____ (practice)
indoors yesterday because it was raining. (Necessity)

10. Rhonda _____ (talk) to her father, but she had too
much pride to admit that she needed his help. (Suggestion)

Modal Auxiliaries – Past Tense (Hard Version)

Directions: Use the correct past tense auxiliary verb to complete each sentence.

Example: Cory didn't make a good grade on his test. He
_____ (study) harder.
Cory didn't make a good grade on his test. He <u>should have</u>
<u>studied</u> harder. (Advisability)

1. Sheldon _____ (finish) his art project because he didn't have enough paint.

2. Greg gave a speech to three hundred people. He _____ (be) nervous in front of so many people.

3. I feel bad. I _____ (help) my friend move to his new house, but I told him I was busy.

4. Ruth _____ (wait) for an hour before she got to see the doctor.

5. Hal _____ (wash) his car yesterday, but it rained.

6. Kate and John are broke. They _____ (save) some money instead of spending every dime they made.

7. Rodney has heartburn. He _____ (eat) too much spicy food at lunch or at dinner.

8. I remember that Mr. Hanson always wore a blue shirt. He _____ (like) the color blue.

9. Dick and Jane _____ (go) to the meeting last night because they didn't have a babysitter for their son.

10. Our backyard is very small. We _____ (buy) a house with a bigger backyard for the children to play.

Conditional Sentences - Rules

A conditional sentence has two clauses, a dependent clause beginning with if and a main clause.

Examples: If you <u>study</u>, you <u>will pass</u> the test.
study = present   will pass = future
(Study now for the test that is in the future.)

If you <u>studied</u>, you <u>would pass</u> the test.
studied = past   would = present/future
(You don't study, so you won't pass the test.)

If you <u>had studied</u>, you <u>would have passed</u> the test.
had studied = past perfect   would have passed = past
(You didn't study, so you didn't pass the test.)

If you <u>study</u>, you <u>pass</u> the test.
study = present   pass = present
(When you study, you pass the test.)

If I <u>were</u> a millionaire, I <u>would retire</u> immediately.
were = past   would retire = present/future
(I am not a millionaire, so I can't retire.)

Special note – In a dependent clause in a conditional sentence, <u>were </u>is used to represent the past tense of the "to be" verb for all subjects.

Example: <u>If</u> Bill <u>were</u> here, he would know what to do.

If the dependent clause comes first, then a comma is needed at the end of the clause.

Example: <u>If it rains tomorrow</u>, we won't go to the beach.

If the main clause comes first, then no comma is needed.

Example: <u>We won't go to the beach</u> if it rains tomorrow.

Conditional Sentences

Directions: Use the correct form of the verb in parentheses to complete the sentence.

Example: If Sharon has enough lemons, she _____ (make) lemonade.
   If Sharon has enough lemons, she <u>will make</u> lemonade.

1.   If Maria _____ (own) a car, she would drive to California.

2.   If I see Blake this afternoon, I _____ (give) him the message.

3.   If the police _____ (stop) Steven, they would have given him a ticket for driving without a license.

4.   If Shelley gets a raise, she _____ (buy) a new car next December.

5.   If Chris _____ (be) sick, he would stay home.

6.   Julie likes to eat chili if the weather _____ (be) cold.

7.   If I _____ (be) tired tonight, I won't go to the party.

8.   If Patricia _____ (listen) to her parents' advice, she wouldn't have made so many mistakes in her life.

9.   If it _____ (be) too hot during the day, I don't work in the yard.

10.   If Gloria spoke English fluently, she _____ (get) a job in a lawyer's office.

More Conditional Sentences

Directions: Read the conditional sentences and then answer the questions with yes or no.

Example: If Kelly goes to the store, he will buy only junk food.
Will Kelly buy any fruits or vegetables? No

1.   If I spoke Spanish, I would move to Costa Rica.
Do I speak Spanish? _____

2.   If Bob were a mechanic, he would fix his own truck.
Can Bob fix his truck when it breaks down? _____

3.   If Melinda has enough time, she will make flan for dessert.
Is Melinda willing to make flan for dessert? _____

4.   Linda answers the phone if she is in her office.
Linda is working in her office when the phone rings. Is she going to answer the phone? _____

5.   If Keith had a million dollars, he would retire immediately.
Is Keith retiring soon? _____

6.   If Ana hadn't gotten sick, she would have gone to the party.
Did Ana get sick before the party? _____

7.   If Lori has enough time, she goes to a movie every week.
Do you think that Lori goes to a movie every week? _____

8.   If I had been smarter, I would have bought a small house when I was in college.
Did I buy a small house when I was in college? _____

9.   If I were Chris, I would tell the truth.
Am I going to tell the truth? _____

10.   If I had a screwdriver, I would fix this machine.
Do I have a screwdriver to fix this machine? _____

And More Conditional Sentences

Directions: Fill in the blank with the correct form of the verb in parentheses to complete the conditional sentence.

Example: If I finish the test quickly, I _____ (go) home early.
           If I finish the test quickly, I <u>will go</u> home early.

1.   If Vickie quits college next semester, it _____ (be) a terrible mistake.

2.   If Mario were wise, he _____ (save) his money.

3.   If Cindy and Mike had known about the ghost, they _____ (purchase) the house.

4.   If Andrea works hard, she _____ (do) well in high school next year.

5.   If Hector works overtime, he _____ (send) the extra money to his parents in El Salvador.

6.   If I had one million dollars, I _____ (buy) a new house in Big Mountain Estates.

7.   If the boys had stayed at the party, they _____ (get) into a fight.

8.   If the boss looks good, we _____ (look) good.

9.   Tracy _____ (admit) her mistake if she were honest.

10. Joe _____ (become) a detective if he had joined the police department.

110

Wish

Wish is used when the speaker wants reality to be different than what it is.

Wish is followed by a noun clause. A noun clause contains a subject and a verb and is used as a subject or an object in a sentence.

Example: Rose heard <u>what George said</u>.

In the example, <u>what George said</u> is a noun clause. It is used as the object of the verb <u>heard</u>.

Past tense forms, similar to those in conditional sentences, are used in the noun clause. For example, <u>would</u>, the past tense of <u>will</u>, is used to make a wish about the future. The simple past is used to make a wish about the present. The past perfect is used to make a wish about the past.

Reality/Future	Verb Form with Wish/Future
They won't help me.	I wish they would help me.
He isn't going to help me.	I wish he were going to help me.
They can't help me.	I wish they could help me.

Reality/Present	Verb Form with Wish/Present
I don't speak French.	I wish I spoke French.
I am studying French.	I wish I weren't studying French.
I can't speak French.	I wish I could speak French.

Reality/Past	Verb Form with Wish/Past
Allen didn't come.	I wish Allen had come.
Allen couldn't come	I wish Allen could have come.

Wish

Directions: Complete the following sentences with the appropriate verb form. <u>Were</u> is used for both singular and plural subjects.

Example: I <u>am living</u> in Texas. (Reality)
          I wish I <u>weren't living</u> in Texas. (Wish)

1.   Our school doesn't have any computers. I wish our school
     _____ (have) some computers.

2.   Pamela didn't go to the movie with me yesterday. I wish she
     _____ (go) to the movie with me yesterday.

3.   Joe won't tell me the truth, but I wish he _____ (tell) me
     the truth.

4.   I could not understand a word that the speaker said. I wish I
     _____ (understand) the speaker because her
     lectures are always interesting.

5.   I am going to go to the meeting on July 23rd. I wish I
     _____ (go) to the meeting on the 23rd.

6.   Noni is living in a very small apartment right now. She wishes she
     _____ (live) in a very small apartment right now.

7.   Bob can't play basketball with us tomorrow. That means we don't
     have enough players to make a team. I wish Bob
     _____ (play) basketball with us tomorrow.

8.   Earl can't afford a new car right now, but he wishes he
     _____ (afford) a new car right now.

9.   Glenn is sick. He wishes he _____ (be) sick.

10. John came to my New Year's Eve party last year. I wish he
     _____ (come) to my party because he drank
     too much and insulted some of my guests.

Wish (#2)

Example: Victor <u>ate</u> six slices of pepperoni pizza. (Reality)
           He wishes he <u>had not eaten</u> six slices of pepperoni pizza.

1.   Elvira <u>isn't</u> here today. I wish she _____ here today.

2.   Magda had a good time in San Antonio last weekend. Paul <u>didn't go</u> with her. He wishes he _____ with Magda to San Antonio.

3.   Janie made a terrible grade on her test. She <u>didn't study</u>. She wishes she _____.

4.   Martha wants to be in the church choir, but she <u>can't sing</u> very well. She wishes she _____ better.

5.   My feet are killing me! I <u>am wearing</u> these uncomfortable dress shoes. I wish I _____ tennis shoes.

6.   That cake looks delicious, but I <u>am</u> on a diet. I wish I _____ on a diet.

7.   Julie always falls asleep during English class. She <u>doesn't get</u> enough sleep at night. She wishes she _____ more sleep at night.

8.   Emilio <u>could not come</u> to class yesterday. He missed an interesting grammar lesson. He wishes he _____ to class yesterday.

9.   Nidia <u>can't attend</u> the graduation ceremony tomorrow. She wishes she _____ the graduation ceremony tomorrow.

10. My wife and I <u>are going to see</u> an art exhibit at the museum. It will be so boring! I wish I _____ an art exhibit at the museum.

One More Wish

Wish suggests a situation that is unreal or contrary to fact.

Example: I wish I <u>could get</u> to work on time. (Wish)
 I <u>can't get</u> to work on time. (Reality)

Directions: Change the wish back to reality.

1. I wish I <u>could have helped</u> Tony.
 But sadly, I _____ Tony.

2. Some days, I wish I <u>had gone</u> to law school.
 When I had the chance, I _____ to law school.

3. I wish I <u>had</u> a lot of money.
 The truth is I _____ a lot of money.

4. I wish I <u>were</u> in Hawaii.
 But here I am in Galena Park. I _____ in Hawaii.

5. I wish I <u>were eating</u> a cheeseburger right now.
 Unfortunately, I _____ a cheeseburger right now.

6. I wish I <u>could speak</u> Japanese.
 I have enough trouble with English. I _____ Japanese.

7. I wish I <u>would learn</u> to play the piano.
 I have no musical ability. I _____ to play the piano.

8. I wish I <u>had</u> twenty GED students.
 Right now, I _____ twenty GED students.

9. I wish I <u>were going to retire</u> next year.
 Unless I win the lottery, I _____ next year.

10. I wish I <u>were</u> thirty years old.
 However, I _____ thirty years old.

Tag Questions – Negative Tag

A tag question asks a question to seek confirmation of an idea that we believe to be true. Tag questions contain a pronoun and an auxiliary verb, but not an action verb. Use a negative tag after an affirmative sentence. Always use a contraction in a negative tag question.

Examples: Vanessa <u>is</u> in the fourth grade, <u>isn't</u> she?
is = positive
isn't = negative

Bob <u>teaches</u> at the college, <u>doesn't</u> he?
teaches = present tense/third person/positive
doesn't = present tense/third person/negative

Directions: Use the correct tag question in the following sentences.

1. You drink coffee every morning, _____?

2. Andrea and Maria are working today, _____?

3. Nancy went on a date last Saturday, _____?

4. Angie can speak English well, _____?

5. Yesterday's weather was beautiful, _____?

6. They have been here before, _____?

7. I should be more patient, _____?

8. Ana and Cecilia are sisters, _____?

9. Mario drives a gray truck, _____?

10. A laptop computer is expensive, _____?

Tag Questions – Affirmative Tag

Use a positive (affirmative) tag question after a negative sentence. Notice that the ending punctuation is a question mark, not a period. Always use a pronoun in the tag question.

Examples: Gerardo <u>isn't</u> married, <u>is</u> he?
Rosalinda <u>hasn't gone</u> to the doctor yet, <u>has</u> she?

Directions: Use the correct tag question in the following sentences.

1. Yolanda doesn't know how to dance, _____?

2. Peter wouldn't give you the information, _____?

3. You didn't study for the test, _____?

4. Keith doesn't eat meat, _____?

5. Jose won't teach summer school next year, _____?

6. Fred isn't working right now, _____?

7. Karla and Javier don't have any children, _____?

8. Gary wasn't happy, _____?

9. William hasn't played tennis in many years, _____?

10. Debra can't speak Russian, _____?

Tag Questions – Review

Use a negative tag question after a positive sentence.
Example: Oscar and Felix <u>will be</u> at the party, <u>won't</u> they?

Use a positive tag question after a negative sentence.
Example: Oscar and Felix <u>won't be</u> at the party, <u>will</u> they?

A comma comes between the sentence and the tag question. If a sentence is positive, then the expected answer is positive. If a sentence is negative, then the expected answer is negative.

Examples: Mike lives in Hawaii, doesn't he?
              Yes, he does.

              Karla didn't do well on the test, did she?
              No, she didn't.

Directions: Use the correct tag question in the following sentences.

1.   Juan has been studying English for two years, _____?

2.   Sally didn't pay her speeding ticket, _____?

3.   Linda is going to be in third grade next year, _____?

4.   They aren't good friends, _____?

5.   Adrianna sits in the front row, _____?

6.   Carmen doesn't like to study algebra, _____?

7.   Jack was absent last Thursday, _____?

8.   I can't go to California with you, _____?

9.   Greg has lived in Argentina for many years, _____?

10.   The children don't look like their mother, _____?

117

Too

In order to avoid repetition of an earlier word or phrase, use <u>too</u> with a subject and an auxiliary verb in a positive (affirmative) sentence. Notice that the sentence with <u>too</u> does not contain a comma.

Example: Marco speaks English, and Margarita <u>speaks</u> English.
Marco speaks English and Margarita <u>does</u> too.
(speaks = present tense/third person/action verb)
(does = present tense/third person/auxiliary verb)

Directions: Shorten the following sentences by using a subject, an auxiliary verb, and <u>too</u>.

1.   Lisa left right after lunch, and Bill left right after lunch.

2.   Dale is going to the concert, and Betty is going to the concert.

3.   Kate will be here at ten o'clock, and I will be here at ten o'clock.

4.   Shelly wants to go there, and Herman wants to go there.

5.   My clock is fast, and your clock is fast.

6.   Sonia is making progress, and Luis is making progress.

7.   Berry was arrested, and his assistant was arrested.

8.   Nancy will be there, and her brother will be there.

9.   We go to the park every day, and they go to the park every day.

10.   Marc can speak French, and Juanita can speak French.

So

In order to avoid repetition of an earlier word or phrase, use <u>so</u> with an auxiliary verb and a subject in a positive (affirmative) sentence.

Example: Marco was sick yesterday, and Marta was sick yesterday.
Marco was sick yesterday and so was Marta.

Directions: Shorten the following sentences by using <u>so</u>, an auxiliary verb, and a subject.

1.   Lisa left right after lunch, and Bill left right after lunch.

2.   Dale is going to the concert, and Betty is going to the concert.

3.   Kate will be here at ten o'clock, and I will be here at ten o'clock.

4.   Shelly wants to go there, and Herman wants to go there.

5.   My clock is fast, and your clock is fast.

6.   Sonia is making progress, and Luis is making progress.

7.   Berry was arrested, and his assistant was arrested.

8.   Nancy will be there, and her brother will be there.

9.   We go to the park every day, and they go to the park every day.

10.   Marc can speak French, and Juanita can speak French.

Either

In order to avoid repetition of an earlier word or phrase, use <u>either</u> with a subject and an auxiliary verb in a negative sentence.

Example: Felix doesn't bowl, and Martha doesn't bowl.
Felix doesn't bowl and Martha doesn't either.

Directions: Shorten the following sentences by using a subject, an auxiliary verb, and <u>either</u>.

1.   Ramon didn't like the movie, and I didn't like the movie.

2.   Jose won't attend the class, and Bill won't attend the class.

3.   Sandy hasn't been to Europe, and Maria hasn't been to Europe.

4.   Margarita can't swim, and Daniel can't swim.

5.   Joe couldn't go to Boston, and Brian couldn't go to Boston.

6.   Dave doesn't have a computer, and we don't have a computer.

7.   Hilda shouldn't quit school, and Erika shouldn't quit school.

8.   Your answer isn't correct, and my answer isn't correct.

9.   I couldn't go to the party, and Barry couldn't go to the party.

10.   Mr. Gallo wasn't in the office, and Mr. Diaz wasn't in the office.

Neither

To avoid repetition of earlier words, use <u>neither</u> with an auxiliary verb and a subject. Neither is negative, so a positive auxiliary verb is used.

Example: Felix doesn't bowl, and Martha <u>doesn't</u> bowl.
Felix doesn't bowl and neither <u>does</u> Martha.

Directions: Shorten the following sentences by using <u>neither</u>, an auxiliary verb, and a subject.

---

1. Ramon didn't like the movie, and I didn't like the movie.

2. Jose won't attend the class, and Bill won't attend the class.

3. Sandy hasn't been to Europe, and Maria hasn't been to Europe.

4. Margarita can't swim, and Daniel can't swim.

5. Jose couldn't go to Boston, and Brian couldn't go to Boston.

6. Dave doesn't have a computer, and we don't have a computer.

7. Hilda shouldn't quit school, and Erika shouldn't quit school.

8. Your answer isn't correct, and my answer isn't correct.

9. I couldn't go to the party, and Barry couldn't go to the party.

10. Mr. Gallo wasn't in the office, and Mr. Diaz wasn't in the office.

Too, So, Either, Neither – Review

Directions: Avoid repetition by using too/so or either/neither.

Examples: Matt's eyes are brown, and Oscar's eyes are brown.
Matt's eyes are brown and Oscar's eyes are too.
Matt's eyes are brown and so are Oscar's eyes.
Mary doesn't eat junk food, and Joe doesn't eat junk food.
Mary doesn't eat junk food and Joe doesn't either.
Mary doesn't eat junk food and neither does Joe.

1.   Javier doesn't play tennis, and Yolanda doesn't play tennis.

2.   Ana didn't enjoy the play, and her son didn't enjoy the play.

3.   Delia saw the movie, and Beth saw the movie.

4.   Myrna hasn't been to Oregon, and Jeff hasn't been to Oregon.

5.   Pat should study for the test, and Kate should study for the test.

6.   Rosa does yoga every day, and Lorena does yoga every day.

7.   Paul has allergies, and I have allergies.

8.   Glenn can't drive a car, and Elvira can't drive a car.

9.   Dana wouldn't lie, and Beatrice wouldn't lie.

10.   Craig is leaving, and we are leaving.

Too, So, Either, Neither – Another Final Review

Directions: Correct the mistakes in the part containing too, so, either, or neither.

Example: Sue lives in Florida and her sister lives too. (Incorrect)
Sue lives in Florida and her sister <u>does</u> too. (Correct)

1.   Mario is working two jobs and so is working Craig.

2.   Vickie isn't married and Brenda is either.

3.   Candelario works very hard, and so does Luis.

4.   My car hasn't been stolen and neither doesn't Greg's car.

5.   I missed the party and Vanessa was too.

6.   Andrew doesn't like sushi and neither doesn't Michelle.

7.   Guillermina was absent yesterday and Theresa was so.

8.   John was living in Utah last year and so was Bill and Avery.

9.   The teacher has two children and so Gloria has too.

10.   We won't go to San Antonio next weekend and they will neither.

Too, So, Either, Neither – Final Review

> Directions: Rewrite the sentences to their full form. Don't forget the comma.

Examples: George went to China and so did Jill.
George went to China, and Jill went to China.
I couldn't hear the radio and Pete couldn't either.
I couldn't hear the radio, and Pete couldn't hear the radio.

1. Gracia is going to go to Mexico next month and so is Oralia.

2. Jesus doesn't drink soda in the morning and Teri doesn't either.

3. Marilyn is sixty one years old and Thelma is too.

4. Teresa can't speak Russian and neither can Lorena.

5. Julian always runs three miles before work and so does Magda.

6. I haven't talked to Melissa and Ely hasn't either.

7. Diana won't listen to your advice and neither will Cecilia.

8. Jason loves to play tennis and Rosalinda does too.

9. My car is silver and so is Patricia's

10. Yolanda's hair is very pretty and Ruth's hair is too.

Too, So, Either, Neither – The Final, Final Review

Directions: Reduce unnecessary repetition, *if possible*, by using too and so or either and neither.

Examples: Max lives in Austin, and Alex lives in Austin.
Max lives in Austin and Alex does too. Or
Max lives in Austin and so does Alex.

Lori isn't hungry right now, and Janice isn't hungry right now.
Lori isn't hungry right now and Janice isn't either. Or
Lori isn't hungry right now and neither is Janice.

Warren likes to play <u>tennis</u>, and Glennis likes to play <u>golf</u>.
(No reduction is possible. Warren and Glennis like different sports.)

1. Bill has a beautiful garden, and Debbie has a beautiful garden.

2. Glenn is asleep, and Linda is asleep.

3. Dale isn't married, and Jimmy isn't married.

4. Brian lives in Ohio, and Keith lives in Nevada.

5. Cristela doesn't drink coffee, and Cesar doesn't drink coffee.

6. Diana won't go to Florida this summer, and Maria won't go to California this summer.

7. Ruth is wearing sandals, and Laura is wearing sandals.

8. Chase's dog is big, and Leah's dog is small.

9. Joey goes to church on Saturday evening, and I go to church on Saturday evening.

10. Adriana drives a white car, and Mariela drives a white truck.

Problem Verbs (Beat vs. Win)

The difference between these frequently misused verbs is that one <u>beats</u> teams or opponents, and one <u>wins</u> competitions, games, or prizes.

Examples: Rafael <u>won</u> **a tennis tournament** last Sunday. (competition)
Rafael <u>beat</u> **Roger** in the finals. (opponent)

Directions: Complete each sentence with the correct form of beat <u>or</u> win.

1. The Russian Army _____ the German Army at the Battle of Stalingrad in 1943.

2. When Bruce and I race, Bruce _____ me every time.

3. Paulina _____ a gold medal in her gymnastics competition last weekend.

4. Mario _____ the lottery next week.

5. The softball game is in the third inning, and Martina's team _____ 3 to 1.

6. Dana _____ an argument with her husband last night.

7. The San Francisco Giants _____ the Houston Astros yesterday.

8. The Astros _____ thirteen games so far this season.

9. Bobby _____ Boris in their last chess match.

10. John F. Kennedy _____ Richard Nixon to become president in the election of 1960.

Problem Verbs (Borrow vs. Lend)

One <u>borrows</u> something from someone, and one <u>lends</u> something to someone.

Examples: Marisa <u>borrowed</u> **my car** because her car wasn't running. (Marisa needed a car, so she borrowed a car.)
Ken <u>lent</u> **one of his tennis rackets to Jimmy** because Jimmy's tennis racket had a broken string. (Ken had an extra tennis racket, so he lent it to Jimmy.)

Directions: Complete the sentence with the correct form of borrow <u>or</u> lend.

1. Can I _____ your dictionary, please? I left my dictionary at home.

2. Can you _____ your phone to me, please? My battery is low.

3. Jose _____ five dollars from Sheila yesterday.

4. Sheila _____ five dollars to Jose yesterday.

5. I need some notebook paper for the math test. _____ me some notebook paper.

6. Dora's son _____ money from her every month, but he never pays her back.

7. Derrick's father _____ never _____ him a dime, and he probably never will.

8. Eddie _____ my pressure washer next Saturday.

9. The United States _____ money from China, Japan, and Saudi Arabia to finance its budget deficit.

10. Ted _____ his truck to Yvonne so that she could go to work.

Problem Verbs (Do vs. Make)

The difference between do and make is idiomatic. Both have the meaning to accomplish or to perform. Some examples are:

<u>Make</u>   <u>Do</u>
a bed   dishes
a meal or food   work
a phone call   exercise
a mistake   homework

Directions: Complete each sentence with the correct form of do <u>or</u> make.

1.   Jose _____ his exercises every day because exercise makes him feel better.

2.   Max and Doris _____ their chores on Saturday so they can relax and have fun on Sunday.

3.   I _____ breakfast every Saturday morning.

4.   Vanessa _____ already _____ her homework.

5.   Catalina _____ a mistake on her job application. She wrote down her maiden name instead of her married name.

6.   Alexis _____ a face when I offered to cook liver and onions for dinner.

7.   Betty _____ all her paperwork before she went on vacation last week.

8.   My wife _____ pancakes every Sunday morning.

9.   Linda and Glenn _____ their beds every morning before they go to school.

10. Shhh! Oralia _____ a very important phone call.

Problem Verbs (Learn vs. Teach)

The difference between learn and teach is that <u>learn</u> means to gain knowledge from someone (a teacher) or from something (a book) while <u>teach</u> means to instruct someone or to cause someone to gain knowledge.

Examples: My uncle <u>taught</u> me <u>to</u> drive. (Teacher = My uncle)
I <u>learned</u> to drive <u>from</u> my uncle. (Student = I)

Directions: Complete each sentence with the correct form of learn <u>or</u> teach.

1.   Good teachers _____ their students to think for themselves.

2.   Roger _____ how to play tennis from his father when he was a young boy.

3.   When Peter lived in Greece, he _____ English by watching American television programs.

4.   Mr. Daugherty _____ us a lot about American history last semester.

5.   Mr. Clark _____ Sunday School since 2002.

6.   Linda is in her bedroom right now. She _____ her lines in the school play.

7.   Last night, Nicole _____ the definitions of her vocabulary words from her new dictionary

8.   My wife _____ our son a few Spanish words.

9.   I just _____ that Esperanza was injured in a car accident.

10.   I _____ how to dance from Ginger next month.

Problem Verbs (Speak vs. Talk)

Speak is used for greetings, languages, and is more formal than talk. *Talk* is used for informal conversations.

Examples: Phil and Maria <u>spoke</u> to the priest about their marital problems.
Bob <u>is talking</u> to his brother about sports.

Directions: Complete each sentence with the correct form of speak <u>or</u> talk.

1.   I _____ to my good friend Keith last night.

2.   Ted _____ to his wife about their vacation plans now.

3.   Juan _____ English well because he practices every day.

4.   Doug _____ at his father's retirement dinner last night.

5.   Shhh! William _____ on the phone with his boss.

6.   Henry _____ with a heavy German accent.

7.   Every day, the president _____ with his economic advisors.

8.   Grace _____ too much during class. She is disruptive.

9.   The manager _____ to the employees tomorrow.

10.   Christina _____ Spanish well because her father didn't permit the language in his house.

Problem Verbs – Review

Directions: Complete the sentence with the correct verb from the list.

beat, borrow, do, learn, lend, make, speak, talk, teach, win

1. Charles _____Spanish very well.

2. I _____ my son to throw a baseball when he was four years old.

3. Raquel _____ already _____ her math homework.

4. _____ you _____ me your lawnmower tomorrow?

5. I _____ Arnold in the weightlifting competition last week.

6. Carol _____ to her mother twice a week.

7. Neil _____ a lot about life from his late uncle.

8. The United States _____ the next World Cup.

9. Priscilla _____ the best homemade macaroni and cheese that I have ever tasted.

10. Paul _____ a tennis racket from me last week, but he hasn't returned it yet.

Gerunds

A gerund is the "ing" form of a verb used as a noun. A gerund is used as a subject, as an object of a verb, or as an object of a preposition.

Examples: <u>Swimming</u> is a great form of exercise. (subject)
I enjoy <u>playing</u> golf. (object of the verb <u>enjoy</u>)
This machine is used for <u>making</u> keys. (object of the preposition <u>for</u>)

Use gerunds after prepositions, but not after <u>to</u> when it is part of an infinitive verb construction.

Example: Linda wants <u>to buy</u> some new shoes. (infinitive verb)

Infinitives

An infinitive is to + the simple form of a verb.

Example: The boss needs <u>to speak</u> with you. (infinitive verb)

An infinitive is used to complete the meaning of some verbs.

Examples: Ellen <u>loves to watch</u> romantic movies. (the infinitive form of watch follows the verb loves)

Some verbs are followed by gerunds. Some verbs are followed by infinitives. Some verbs can be followed by gerunds or infinitives.

Examples: Lety <u>went</u> **shopping** yesterday.

I <u>hope</u> **to see** you next Friday.

Rosalinda <u>likes</u> **playing** tennis.

Rosalinda <u>likes</u> **to play** tennis.

Gerunds and Infinitives

Verbs followed by gerunds
appreciate
avoid
consider
delay
discuss
enjoy
finish (get through)
go (recreational activities)
keep (keep on)
mention
mind
postpone (put off)
suggest
quit (give up)

Verbs followed by either a gerund or an infinitive with no difference in meaning
begin
can't bear
can't stand
continue
hate
like
love
prefer
start

Verbs followed by either a gerund or an infinitive with a difference in meaning
forget
regret
remember
try

Verbs followed by infinitives
agree
appear
ask
decide
expect
hope
intend
need
offer
plan
pretend
promise
refuse
seem
want
would like

Verb + noun + infinitive
advise
allow
encourage
force
invite
permit
order
remind
require
tell
warn

Gerunds and Infinitives

Directions: Use the gerund or the infinitive form of the verb in parentheses to complete each sentence.

Example: Donald refused _____ the truth. (tell)
           Donald **refused** to tell the truth. (refused = clue word)

1.   We have finished _____ our living room. (paint)

2.   Maureen would like _____ Tom in the office. (see)

3.   The school requires students _____ a uniform. (wear)

4.   _____ is a good way to stay in shape. (swim)

5.   I plan _____ with the owner about my refund. (speak)

6.   He wants _____ to the party. (come)

7.   Do you mind _____ the baby's diaper? (change)

8.   Glenn goes _____ with his son every Friday. (fish)

9.   A receptionist needs _____ the phone. (answer)

10.   Sue made her family proud by _____ school. (finish)

Gerunds and Infinitives (#2)

Directions: Use the gerund <u>or</u> the infinitive form of the verb in parentheses to complete each sentence.

1. Paulina began _____ GED class last year. (take)

2. Kyle likes _____ documentaries about World War II. (watch)

3. My friends considered _____ their house to pay off debt. (sell)

4. Linda promised _____ her new dog. (take care of)

5. The quarterback continued _____ after his knee injury. (run)

6. Ted quit _____ after his third heart attack. (smoke)

7. The men kept _____ despite the bad weather. (work)

8. Roger loves _____ tennis. (play)

9. Melinda and John would like _____ a new house this year. (buy)

10. They have decided _____ until next year. (wait)

Gerunds and Infinitives (#3)

Directions: Use the gerund or the infinitive form of the verb in parentheses to complete each sentence.

1. I enjoy _____ cartoons with my children on Saturday morning. (watch)

2. Emilio and Guadalupe plan _____ to a new house next year. (move)

3. Sheila agreed _____ an ESL class in the afternoon. (teach)

4. The police ordered the man _____. (stop)

5. Claude and Alberto are going to go _____ in Italy next January. (ski)

6. Dave suggested _____ two years before buying a new house. (wait)

7. I can't stand _____ to my mother when she complains about her friends. (listen)

8. Dan hates _____ in Houston traffic. (drive)

9. My wife reminded me _____ the dishwasher. (unload)

10. Ron has finally finished _____ Joshua Pope's latest novel. (read)

Gerunds and Infinitives – Forget, Regret, Remember, and Try

Forget, regret, remember, and try can be followed by either a gerund or an infinitive. However, the meaning is different.

Forget + gerund = forget something that happened in the past.

Example: I will never <u>forget seeing</u> my daughter for the first time.

Forget + infinitive = forget to perform a responsibility or duty.

Example: Linda often <u>forgets to put</u> her dirty clothes in the hamper.

Regret + gerund = regret something that happened in the past.

Example: Sally <u>regrets losing</u> contact with her best friend.

Regret + infinitive = regret to tell someone bad news.

Example: I <u>regret to tell</u> you that your puppy has run away.

Remember + gerund = remember something that happened in the past.

Example: Don <u>remembers meeting</u> his wife in 1932.

Remember + infinitive = remember to perform a responsibility or duty.

Example: Mindy always <u>remembers to set</u> the alarm.

Try + gerund = try a different way.

Example: Because the students failed the first algebra test, the teacher <u>tried explaining</u> in Spanish.

Try + infinitive = make an effort

Example: Lisa is <u>trying to lose</u> weight.

Gerunds and Infinitives – Forget, Regret, Remember, and Try

> Directions: Fill in the blank with the gerund or the infinitive form of the verb in parentheses.

1. I remember _____ my first paycheck at the tender age of sixteen. (receive)

2. Louis forgot _____ milk at the grocery store. (buy)

3. Greg is trying _____ a better father. (become)

4. Debbie regrets _____ her son a new car. He has become a spoiled brat. (get)

5. I regret _____ you that your credit card has been cancelled. (inform)

6. Brett forgot _____ the winning touchdown because of his concussion. (score)

7. My uncle remembers _____ his rent on the first of each month. (pay)

8. My son won't take his medicine. I tried _____ it in chocolate pudding, but that didn't fool him. (put)

9. I forgot _____ the garage door this morning. (close)

10. The students are trying _____. (concentrate)

Gerunds and Infinitives – Forget, Regret, Remember, and Try (#2)

Directions: Fill in the blank with the gerund <u>or</u> the infinitive form of the verb in parentheses.

1. Harvey regrets _____ his wife about his past indiscretions because now she wants a divorce. (tell)

2. Maya remembers _____ in Peru as a small child. (live)

3. Luke regretted _____ four spicy tacos right before bed last night. (eat)

4. John has tried _____ a job since January. (find)

5. Jackie forgot _____ out the trash this morning. His wife is going to be angry. (take)

6. I remembered _____ a doctor's appointment for Sybil for Friday. (make)

7. First, Pam listened to soothing sounds on her radio. Then, she tried _____ sheep, but she couldn't get to sleep. (count)

8. I regret _____ that I need to lose weight. (admit)

9. Elvira has tried _____ biting her fingernails. (quit)

10. Jean regrets _____ her son when he was a baby. (spank)

Gerunds and Infinitives – Prefer

Prefer has a special form when used with a gerund or an infinitive.

Examples: I <u>prefer renting</u> a movie **to going** to a theater.
I <u>prefer to rent</u> a movie **rather than to go** to a theater.
I <u>prefer to rent</u> a movie **than go** to a theater.
(<u>Rather</u> and <u>to</u> are optional in this form.)

Directions: Fill in the blank with the gerund <u>or</u> the infinitive form of the verb in parentheses.

1.   The customers preferred _____ a refund to getting a rain check. (receive)

2.   I prefer _____ for a table to going to another restaurant. (wait)

3.   Alan prefers _____ golf than play tennis. (play)

4.   Tim would prefer _____ the grass rather than to sweep the clippings. (mow)

5.   Michelle prefers _____ to running. (walk)

6.   My family prefers _____ home for dinner than eat at a restaurant. (stay)

7.   Natasha prefers _____ her car to taking a plane when she travels to Dallas. (drive)

8.   On the other hand, Natasha's husband prefers _____ rather than drive his car when he travels to Dallas. (fly)

9.   My children prefer _____ television to cleaning their rooms. (watch)

10. Bertha prefers _____ a steak than eat sushi. (eat)

Gerunds and Infinitives – Review

Directions: Complete each sentence with the gerund or the infinitive form of the verb in parentheses.

1. Did you remember _____ the door? (lock)

2. Jennifer avoids _____ with her ex-husband because he has a bad temper. (talk)

3. Bertha began _____ piano lessons last summer. (take)

4. The professor doesn't allow her students _____ the classroom during an exam. (leave)

5. Ted went _____ with his uncle last November. (hunt)

6. Melinda prefers _____ cooking shows rather than to cook. (watch)

7. I want _____ progress in your reading scores. (see)

8. Elizabeth is going to try _____ more patient. (be)

9. Dave always tells Brian _____ more money. (save)

10. Alex refused _____ his brother. (help)

Participial Adjectives (ed vs. ing)

The past participle (ed) and the present participle (ing) can be used as adjectives. The past participle describes how a person feels. The feeling is caused by someone or something. The present participle describes a reason for the feeling.

Examples: Jack and Barbara are watching a golf tournament.
Barbara is <u>bored</u>. Why?
Golf is <u>boring</u> to Barbara.

Directions: Complete each sentence with the present participle (ing) <u>or</u> the past participle (ed) form of the word in parentheses.

1. The governor had an affair with his secretary. The affair was
    _____. (shock)

2. The residents of the state were _____ (shock) by
    the governor's actions.

3. I am _____ (excite) about the game tonight.

4. The game is going to be _____. (excite)

5. I thought I didn't have any money. I was _____
    (surprise) to find fifty dollars in my wallet.

6. Finding fifty dollars was _____ (surprise) to me.

7. Falling out of the boat was very _____
    (embarrass) for John.

8. John was _____ (embarrass) when he fell
    out of the boat.

9. Sue's instructions were _____ (confuse) to her students.

10. Sue's students were _____ (confuse) by her
    instructions.

Participial Adjectives (#2)

The present participle (ing) shows the cause of a feeling.

Example: **Listening to my teacher's stories** is <u>tiring</u>.

The past participle (ed) shows the receiver of the feeling.

Example: I am <u>tired</u> of listening to my teacher's stories.

Directions: Complete each sentence with the present participle <u>or</u> the past participle form of the word in parentheses.

1. The little boy was _____ (frighten) when he heard a strange noise.

2. A strange noise in the middle of the night can be _____ (frighten) for a young child.

3. Phone calls from telemarketers are _____. (annoy)

4. I get _____ (annoy) when telemarketers call my house.

5. Many Americans are _____ (alarm) by the violence in Mexico.

6. The amount that Larry owes on his credit cards is _____. (alarm)

7. The sight of a bird covered in oil is _____. (depress)

8. John and Eric are _____ (depress) because they are unemployed.

9. Bertha feels _____ (relax) around her boss.

10. Doing yoga is _____. (relax)

Review

1. The kitchen floor was sweeped by Veronica last night.
    (Passive Voice)

2. I think that Claude's leg is broken. He is screaming because of the terrible pain. We should take him to the emergency room. (Modal Auxiliaries)

3. If Clarence was younger, he would go to law school. (Conditional Sentences)

4. Lindsey wish she had attended Ashley's graduation ceremony. (Wish)

5. Natasha speaks Russian, can't she? (Tag Questions)

6. Maria left work at 4:30 and Juana did so. (Too, So)

7. Paul hasn't passed the test and neither hasn't Alma. (Either, Neither)

8. They go to shop at the mall once a month. (Gerunds and Infinitives)

9. My uncle learned me how to swim. (Problem Verbs)

10. Young children are boring when they have to sit for a long time. (Participial Adjectives)

Final Review

Directions: Fill in the blank with the correct form of the word in parentheses.

1. We were _____ (disappoint) by the movie.

2. I would rather have _____ (fix) dinner than cleaned the kitchen.

3. If Toby gets a raise next year, he _____ (buy) a new car.

4. For some strange reason, I can't relax. I wish I _____. (relax)

5. Alma isn't scared of insects, _____ (be) she?

6. We were going to go to the beach yesterday and so _____ (be) Jill.

7. The yoga class hasn't been cancelled and the spinning class _____ (have) either.

8. Maxine refused _____ (tip) the waiter for his terrible service.

9. Lee _____ (beat) Robert in their next golf game.

10. Gloria took all five GED tests yesterday. She was _____ (exhaust) last night.

Answer Key – Part I

(Page 1 Present Tense/To Be Verb) 1. is 2. am 3. are 4. is 5. is 6. are 7. is 8. are 9. is 10. is

(Page 2 Present Tense/To Be/Negative Form) 1. is not/isn't 2. is not/isn't 3. are not/aren't 4. is not/isn't 5. is not/isn't 6. are not/aren't 7. are not/aren't 8. is not/isn't 9. am not/I'm not 10. are not/aren't

(Page 3 Present Tense/To Be/Question Form) 1. Is Linda's pencil box blue? 2. Are the dogs friendly? 3. Am I stubborn? 4. Is Glenn three years old? 5. Are Alma and Bertha from Mexico? 6. Is the music too loud? 7. Are Elizabeth and Richard married? 8. Is the food at that restaurant delicious? 9. Are they hungry? 10. Am I always late?

(Page 5 Present Tense/Action Verbs) 1. lives 2. live 3. wants 4. needs 5. like 6. washes 7. go 8. buy 9. rides 10. talks

(Page 6 Present Tense/Action Verbs/Negative Form) 1. Miguel does not/doesn't have a new baby. 2. She does not/doesn't drink coffee every morning. 3. I do not/don't have a headache. 4. They do not/don't eat at a restaurant every Saturday night. 5. We do not/don't watch television every night. 6. Sheila does not/doesn't speak Chinese. 7. Joanie does not/doesn't want a cheese pizza. 8. Sebastian does not/doesn't drive a red truck. 9. You do not/don't work at a shoe store. 10. Linda does not/doesn't walk to school every day.

(Page 7 Present Tense Verbs/Negative Form) 1. Jim does not/doesn't like his new job. 2. Pedro is not/isn't married to Daniela. 3. He does not/doesn't exercise every day. 4. Art does not/doesn't have a beard. 5. Melinda and Joe do not/don't work together. 6. Dave does not/doesn't live in an apartment. 7. The washer is not/isn't broken. 8. The tires are not/aren't new. 9. They do not/don't have three children. 10. The keys are not/aren't lost.

(Page 8 Present Tense/Action Verbs/Question Form) 1. Does Emilio speak Portuguese? 2. Does the class study grammar every day? 3. Do I have two children? 4. Do Sara and Todd run three miles every morning? 5. Does Karl eat oatmeal for breakfast? 6. Does Cesar have a new car? 7. Do many people go grocery shopping on Saturday afternoon? 8. Does Sheila want a cup of coffee? 9. Do you like this kind of music? 10. Does Avery wash her car once a week?

(Page 9 Past Tense/To Be) 1. was 2. were 3. were 4. were 5. was 6. were 7. were 8. was 9. was 10. was

(Page 14 Past Tense/Action Verbs)) 1. bought 2. studied 3. played 4. wrote 5. broke 6. wore 7. graduated 8. got 9. drank 10. washed

(Page 15 Past Tense/To Be and Action Verbs/Negative Form) 1. Alex was not/wasn't sick yesterday. 2. We did not/didn't work in the yard last Saturday. 3. Bud did not/didn't go to Las Vegas in December. 4. They did not/didn't eat spaghetti for dinner last night. 5. We were not/weren't married in 1995. 6. You did not/didn't see my wife at the grocery store. 7. I did not/didn't need aspirin for my headache. 8. Mario did not/didn't have two cups of coffee this morning. 9. We did not/didn't reach our goals. 10. Elsy and Guillermina were not/weren't absent four days ago.

Answer Key – Part I

(Page 16 Past Tense Verbs/Questions) 1. Was Sara a good tennis player? 2. Was Keith a bad employee? 3. Were they friendly with each other? 4. Was Friday a very nice day? 5. Were Martha and Adrianna from Mexico? 6. Were the exercises in Chapter One easy? 7. Was I busy on Thursday night? 8. Were Felix and his wife compassionate with the young woman? 9. Were both windows closed? 10. Were we upset by the terrible news?

(Page 17 Past Tense/Questions) 1. Did Arturo have a mustache last year? 2. Did Margarita go to Canada in June? 3. Was Luis a doctor in El Salvador? 4. Did Julie make several mistakes on her test? 5. Were we surprised to see Julio at the party? 6. Was Gerald correct about his predictions for 2008? 7. Did Larry run five miles yesterday morning? 8. Did Pamela build a new house in 2006? 9. Did Arnoldo lose his job at the warehouse? 10. Was Lupe late for her shift at the hospital last night?

(Page 18 Past Tense Review/Part I) 1. Yes, the students worked well together. 2. Yes, Patricia wore a black dress to the funeral. 3. Yes, the teachers were angry about the boss' decision. 4. Yes, he was at work yesterday. 5. Yes, Felix got a new watch for Christmas. 6. Yes, Lisa went to the dentist this morning. 7. Yes, the food was hot. 8. Yes, the class was ready for the quiz. 9. Yes, Maria seemed upset. 10. Yes, I broke your pencil.

(Page 18 Past Tense Review/Part II) 1. No, the students did not/didn't work well together. 2. No, Patricia did not/didn't wear a black dress to the funeral. 3. No, the teachers were not/weren't angry about the boss' decision. 4. No, he was not/wasn't at work yesterday. 5. No, Felix did not/didn't get a new watch for Christmas. 6. No, Lisa did not/didn't go to the dentist this morning. 7. No, the food was not/wasn't hot. 8. No, the class was not/wasn't ready for the quiz. 9. No, Maria did not/didn't seem upset. 10. No, I did not/didn't break your pencil.

(Page 19 Future Tense) 1. will win/are going to win 2. is going to go 3. will answer 4. is going to retire 5. will get 6. is going to wash 7. will rain/is going to rain 8. are going to sell 9. will help 10. are going to deposit

(Page 20 Future Tense/Negative Form) 1. The Houston Texans will not/won't win the Super Bowl next season. 2. Bob is not/isn't going to teach tennis next June. 3. Peter is not/isn't going to buy a new car next December. 4. I will not/won't help you next weekend. 5. They are not/aren't going to go to San Antonio on Saturday. 6. We will not/won't win the lottery very soon. 7. Betty is not/isn't going to go to the doctor Thursday. 8. You will not/won't pick Hannah up at school on Friday. 9. Nannette will not/won't follow us to the store. 10. You are not/aren't going to be sorry about the decisions that you are making.

(Page 21 Future Tense/Questions) 1. Will the U. S. economy recover soon? 2. Is William going to start his own business next year? 3. Are they going to sign the contract tomorrow? 4. Will the meeting be over by two o'clock? 5. Am I going to move to Bay Oaks in three years? 6. Is Melinda going to fly to Los Angeles on Monday? 7. Is Steven going to study business in college? 8. Will Vanessa become a very good tennis player? 9. Is Raquel going to begin piano lessons in April? 10. Will the professor start his lecture at 7:00?

(Page 22 Simple Tense Review/Present, Past, and Future Part I) 1. Yes, they are going to work in the garden this weekend. 2. Yes, it will rain on Friday. 3. Yes, Penelope and Kris have a cat. 4. Yes, it smells like wet dog in Bud's bedroom. 5. Yes, Natasha spoke to the class. 6. Yes, they were happy to see Jack. 7. Yes, I watched the speech on television last night. 8. Yes, Julie is going to be the new boss. 9. Yes, Julie is the new boss. 10. Yes, I will do you a favor.

(Page 22 Simple Tense Review/Present, Past, and Future Part II) 1. No, they are not/aren't going to work in the garden this weekend. 2. No, it will not/won't rain on Friday. 3. No, Penelope and Kris do not/don't have a cat. 4. No, it does not/doesn't smell like wet dog in Bud's bedroom. 5. No, Natasha did not/didn't speak to the class. 6. No, they were not/weren't happy to see Jack. 7. No, I did not/didn't watch the speech on television last night. 8. No, Julie is not/isn't going to be the new boss. 9. No, Julie is not/isn't the new boss. 10. No, I will not/won't do you a favor.

(Page 23 Simple Verb Tenses/Present, Past, and Future/Sentence Correction) 1. The students took a test last Friday. 2. What are you going to do after class tomorrow? 3. Lindsay and Catherine weren't happy with the test results. 4. Where did you go yesterday? 5. I didn't tell Martha your secret. 6. Mrs. Smith doesn't drive a blue car. 7. You are going to work late on Saturday. 8. Does Cynthia work at a pizza restaurant? 9. The printer doesn't have enough ink to make copies. 10. Did you get a haircut a few days ago?

(Page 25 Present Progressive Verb Tense) 1. is fighting 2. is living 3. is listening 4. are taking 5. is paying 6. is arguing 7. am tying 8. is running 9. are playing 10. is riding

(Page 27 Progressive and Stative Verbs) 1. know 2. is having 3. belongs 4. needs 5. recognize 6. owes 7. contains 8. is talking 9. feel _or_ are feeling 10. is thinking

(Page 28 Present vs. Present Progressive) 1. is watching 2. watches 3. go 4. am going 5. eats 6. is wearing 7. is raining 8. rains 9. lives _or_ is living 10. are chasing

(Page 29 Present or Present Progressive) 1. is reading 2. reads 3. travel 4. is washing 5. washes 6. sings 7. is taking 8. plays 9. are trying 10. cuts

(Page 30 Present Progressive/Negative Form) 1. Angelica is not/isn't reading a book. 2. She does not/doesn't read a book every month. 3. Fidel and Elvira do not/don't travel to Mexico twice a year. 4. Betty is not/isn't washing her car now. 5. She does not/doesn't wash it every weekend. 6. Eddie does not/doesn't like country music. 7. Vanessa is not/isn't taking piano lessons. 8. Raquel does not/doesn't play soccer on Saturday morning. 9. The students are not/aren't concentrating on their work. 10. My mother is not/isn't eighty years old.

(Page 31 Present Progressive/Questions) 1. Are you learning grammar in your English class? 2. Is Sheila beating Tim in their chess game? 3. Is Leroy wearing a gray suit to his job interview tomorrow? 4. Is Deborah cleaning the table? 5. Are Chris and Roxanne watching a movie in the den? 6. Are we meeting with a lawyer this afternoon? 7. Are Joe's brothers serving in the U. S. Navy? 8. Are our neighbors selling their house? 9. Is the boss attending a conference in Dallas next week? 10. Is Cynthia leaving next Friday?

(Page 32 Present Progressive/Questions) 1. Are you going to the store today? 2. Are they renting a house in Clear Lake? 3. Is Felix changing a flat tire? 4. Is Bertha answering an e-mail from her sister? 5. Are Rosalinda and Harriet working at an elementary school? 6. Does Mirna work at a daycare center? 7. Is Mindy from Vietnam? 8. Does Yolanda have two dogs? 9. Does the teacher like Mexican food? 10. Is the soda machine in the hallway working now?

(Page 33 Present or Present Progressive/Questions Part I) 1. Yes, I am studying for the GED. 2. Yes, Luis wears glasses. 3. Yes, they are in a big hurry. 4. Yes, Margarita is wearing a red jacket. 5. Yes, Nadia has long hair. 6. Yes, Leticia is at home. 7. Yes, I have children. 8. Yes, the students are taking a test. 9. Yes, I like fast-food. 10. Yes, she is nervous about her upcoming wedding.

(Page 33 Present or Present Progressive/Questions Part II) 1. No, I am/I'm not studying for the GED. 2. No, Luis does not/doesn't wear glasses. 3. No, they are not/aren't in a big hurry. 4. No, Margarita is not/isn't wearing a red jacket. 5. No, Nadia does not/doesn't have long hair. 6. No, Leticia is not/isn't at home. 7. No, I do not/don't have children. 8. No, the students are not/aren't taking a test. 9. No, I do not/don't like fast-food. 10. No, she is not/isn't nervous about her upcoming wedding.

(Page 34 Past Progressive Verb Tense) 1. were eating 2. was raining 3. was taking 4. were traveling 5. was getting 6. was living 7. was climbing 8. was raining 9. was studying 10. was talking

(Page 35 Past vs. Past Progressive) 1. ate 2. rained 3. took 4. ruined 5. got 6. was playing 7. was taking 8. was driving 9. was shopping 10. was studying

(Page 36 Past Progressive/Negative Form) 1. Roger was not/wasn't studying at the library last night. 2. When his wife called, Emilio was not/wasn't working. 3. On June 26, 2008, I was not/wasn't living in Japan. 4. You were not/weren't talking after the test began. 5. The children were not/weren't lying to their mother. 6. Sue was not/wasn't swimming in the pool when her nose started to bleed. 7. Bert was not/wasn't waiting at a stoplight when another driver hit his car. 8. When it started to rain, Bertha was not/wasn't playing in the park. 9. Snake was not/wasn't riding his motorcycle when the police officer stopped him. 10. Pat was not/wasn't watching a movie when his wife came home.

(Page 37 Past Progressive/Negative Form/#2) 1. Dave was not/wasn't taking a shower when the fire alarm went off. 2. Jose did not/didn't leave a bottle of water in his classroom. 3. Shelly did not/didn't buy ten boxes of Girl Scout cookies. 4. At four o'clock on Saturday afternoon, I was not/wasn't mowing my yard. 5. Felix was not/wasn't feeling well last night. 6. Felix did not/didn't feel well last night. 7. The food at the Japanese restaurant was not/wasn't good. 8. Paula did not/didn't read two books last month. 9. Paula was not/wasn't reading a book when Hugo got home from work. 10. Homer and Lynn were not/weren't at his sister's house last Friday night.

Answer Key – Part I

(Page 38 Past Progressive/Question Form) 1. Was Sharon writing an essay when the electricity suddenly went out? 2. Were Theodore and Sandy getting off the school bus when we drove by? 3. When the war started, was Dale living in Iraq? 4. Was Sophia eating her lunch when the boss came? 5. Was Natasha talking to Joseph when he had a heart attack? 6. Were they having a good time when Charles showed up? 7. When you telephoned, was Robert eating dinner? 8. Were the boys playing basketball in the driveway when Mindy arrived? 9. Was Hilda traveling in Greece on September 11th, 2001? 10. Was a police officer questioning a witness when two detectives arrived?

(Page 39 Past vs. Past Progressive/Questions Part I) 1. Yes, Marcia was shopping when her new car was stolen. 2. Yes, Dana was asleep when I arrived. 3. Yes, they were eating dinner when the telephone rang. 4. Yes, I tried Janeth's spinach empanadas. 5. Yes, Josefa was fired from the store. 6. Yes, my baby was taking a nap when the salesman knocked at the door. 7. Yes, Debbie was cooking dinner when the fire started. 8. Yes, Flora and Cynthia were absent last Friday. 9. Yes, Gabriela was driving when the accident happened. 10. Yes, Andrew broke his arm at work.

(Page 39 Past vs. Past Progressive/Questions Part II) 1. No, Marcia was not/wasn't shopping when her new car was stolen. 2. No, Dana was not/wasn't asleep when I arrived. 3. No, they were not/weren't eating dinner when the telephone rang. 4. No, I did not/didn't try Janeth's empanadas. 5. No, Josefa was not/wasn't fired from the store. 6. No, my baby was not/wasn't taking a nap when the salesman knocked at the door. 7. No, Debbie was not/wasn't cooking dinner when the fire started. 8. No, Flora and Cynthia were not/weren't absent last Friday. 9. No, Gabriela was not/wasn't driving when the accident happened. 10. No, Andrew did not/didn't break his arm at work.

(Page 40 Future Progressive Verb Tense) 1. will be washing 2. will be waiting 3. will be cooking 4. is 5. will be driving 6. will be relaxing 7. will be coming 8. will be enjoying 9. will be visiting 10. will be taking

(Page 41 Future Progressive/Negative Form) 1. Roger will not/won't be studying at the library tomorrow night. 2. When his wife calls, Emilio will not/won't be working. 3. Glenn will not/won't be living in Japan at this time next year. 4. You will not/won't be talking after the test begins. 5. Fred will not/won't be playing in the yard when his mother comes home. 6. Sue will not/won't be swimming in the pool later this afternoon. 7. Bert will not/won't be waiting in his car when you get out of school. 8. Maricela will not/won't be visiting her relatives in Argentina this summer. 9. When his children get home, Viper will not/won't be working on his motorcycle. 10. Pam will not/won't be watching a movie when her mother comes home.

(Page 42 Future Progressive/Questions) 1. Will Sharon be doing her homework later tonight? 2. Will Theodore and Sandy be getting off the school bus at two o'clock? 3. When the war starts, will Dale be living in Mexico? 4. Will Sophia be eating her lunch when the boss comes? 5. Will Dr. McGregor be talking to Joseph about his heart attack? 6. Will Steven be learning Japanese while he is living in Tokyo? 7. Will Roberta be preparing snacks when her guests arrive? 8. Will Hilda be traveling in Greece on July 4th? 9. Will Bob and Brent be playing tennis while Mindy is studying? 10. Will the police be writing tickets for school zone speeders tomorrow morning?

Answer Key – Part I

(Page 43 Progressive Tenses/Positive, Negative, and Question Forms Part I) 1. is not/isn't driving 2. was not/wasn't cooking 3. are not/aren't visiting 4. was not/wasn't wearing 5. will not/won't be taking 6. will not/won't be taking 7. is not/isn't eating 8. were not/weren't living 9. am not/I'm not telling 10. will not/won't be meeting

(Page 43 Progressive Tenses/Positive, Negative, and Question Forms Part II) 1. Is Janeth driving a green car? 2. Was Angelica cooking dinner when the doorbell rang? 3. Are Dolores and Cynthia visiting relatives in Mexico? 4. Was Jose wearing blue jeans on Friday? 5. Will Sandra and Karen be taking a GED test next month? 6. Will Catalina be taking her GED test in February? 7. Is Maria eating a cookie right now? 8. Were they living in California last year? 9. Am I telling a joke to Juanita? 10. Will the class be meeting on Saturday morning?

(Page 44 Present, Future, or Future Progressive) 1. stops 2. is 3. is going to finish 4. is going to take 5. am going to walk 6. will be sleeping 7. will drive 8. is going to go 9. admit 10. is going to travel

(Page 45 Progressive Tense Review) 1. is drinking 2. were talking 3. will be testing 4. was taking 5. was shopping 6. will be visiting 7. is kissing 8. will be spending 9. am trying 10. was soaking

(Page 46 Progressive Verb Tense Review) 1. won't 2. Will Guadalupe be taking GED classes next fall? 3. cooking 4. Are Felix and Martha studying grammar right now? 5. Karen will be going to college after she receives her GED. 6. arguing 7. When the teacher walked into the room, Patricia was talking to Bertha. 8. Sandra was wearing a white shirt yesterday. 9. Oralia is selling jewelry as a part-time job. 10. Who will be teaching the class next week?

(Page 47 Simple and Progressive Verb Tense Review Part I) 1. Yes, I have four children. 2. Yes, I was living in Galveston when the hurricane hit. 3. Yes, Felix is wearing a purple shirt. 4. Yes, I am going to attend the GED class next fall. 5. Yes, Angela was upset by her son's poor grades. 6. Yes, Arturo will be attending the ESL class at this time next year. 7. Yes, Bertha likes her new house. 8. Yes, the baby's diaper is dirty. 9. Yes, Maricela studied for the test. 10. Yes, Janeth likes sushi.

(Page 47 Simple and Progressive Verb Tense Review Part II) 1. No, I do not/don't have four children 2. No, I was not/wasn't living in Galveston when the hurricane hit. 3. No, Felix is not/isn't wearing a purple shirt. 4. No, I am/I'm not going to attend the GED class next fall. 5. No, Angela was not/wasn't upset by her son's poor grades. 6. No, Arturo will not/won't be attending the ESL class at this time next year. 7. No, Bertha does not/doesn't like her new house. 8. No, the baby's diaper is not/isn't dirty. 9. No, Maricela did not/didn't study for the test. 10. No, Janeth does not/doesn't like sushi.

(Page 48 Present Perfect Verb Tense) 1. have already eaten 2. has finished 3. have lived 4. have been 5. has finally done 6. has worked 7. have seen 8. has already left 9. has paid 10. has studied

Answer Key – Book 1

(Page 49 Present Perfect/#2) 1. has taught 2. has driven 3. have dined 4. have been 5. has had 6. have completed 7. has begun 8. has come 9. has run 10. has watched

(Page 50 Past vs. Present Perfect) 1. wrote 2. have heard 3. borrowed 4. began 5. has been 6. have had **or** had 7. brought 8. has lived **or** lived 9. has worked 10. took

(Page 51 Present Perfect/Negative Form) Change the auxiliary verb to the negative form. The main verb doesn't change. 1. has not/hasn't 2. have not/haven't 3. have not/haven't 4. has not/hasn't 5. has not/hasn't 6. have not/haven't 7. has not/hasn't 8. have not/haven't 9. has not/hasn't 10. has not/hasn't

(Page 52 Present Perfect/Questions) 1. <u>Has</u> Frank <u>gone</u> to the doctor yet? 2. <u>Have</u> they <u>sold</u> their house? 3. How long <u>has</u> Bob <u>had</u> a beard? 4. <u>Have</u> you <u>paid</u> your taxes yet? 5. When <u>has</u> she ever <u>been</u> nice to me? 6. Why <u>have</u> we <u>tolerated</u> Lucia's behavior for so long? 7. <u>Have</u> you ever <u>been</u> to Italy? 8. What <u>have</u> they <u>learned</u> in Kindergarten? 9. How long <u>have</u> you <u>lived</u> in Houston? 10. <u>Has</u> Allan <u>finished</u> his assignment?

(Page 53 Present Perfect vs. Past/Questions Part I) 1. Yes, Jose has found a job. 2. Yes, Dorothy went to Corpus Christi last week. 3. Yes, Sandy was sick yesterday. 4. Yes, Frank has seen the doctor about his headaches. 5. Yes, they were happy in their old neighborhood. 6. Yes, Lucy went to college. 7. Yes, Esperanza has finished her essay. 8. Yes, Linda lost a library book last month. 9. Yes, I have spoken to my supervisor about her rude comments. 10. Yes, Magda was a good student.

(Page 53 Present Perfect vs. Past/Questions Part II) 1. No, Jose has not/hasn't found a job. 2. No, Dorothy did not/didn't go to Corpus Christi last week. 3. No, Sandy was not/wasn't sick yesterday. 4. No, Frank has not/hasn't seen the doctor about his headaches. 5. No, they were not/weren't happy in their old neighborhood. 6. No, Lucy did not/didn't go to college. 7. No, Esperanza has not/hasn't finished her essay. 8. No, Linda did not/didn't lose a library book last month. 9. No, I have not/haven't spoken to my supervisor about her rude comments. 10. No, Magda was not/wasn't a good student.

(Page 55 Past Perfect) 1. had done 2. had finished 3. had eaten 4. had set 5. had cleaned 6. had milked 7. had completed 8. had taken 9. had stopped 10. had left

(Page 56 Past Perfect/Negative Form) 1. had not/hadn't eaten 2. had not/hadn't stopped 3. had not/hadn't seen 4. had not/hadn't seen 5. had not/hadn't left 6. had not/hadn't done 7. had not/hadn't started 8. had not/hadn't bought 9. had not/hadn't run 10. had not/hadn't studied

Answer Key – Part I

(Page 57 Past Perfect/Questions) 1. <u>Has</u> the teacher ever <u>been</u> to Puerto Rico? 2. <u>Had</u> Emily <u>visited</u> Japan before she took the trip to Tokyo last year? 3. What <u>had</u> Felix <u>eaten</u> before he got food poisoning? 4. When <u>did</u> Felix <u>get</u> food poisoning? 5. Where <u>have</u> you <u>been</u>? 6. How long <u>has</u> she <u>studied</u> English? 7. <u>Had</u> Bill <u>become</u> a millionaire before he turned thirty? 8. <u>Had</u> the children <u>learned</u> English by the time they came to the United States? 9. <u>Did</u> Martha and her son <u>enjoy</u> the concert last Saturday? 10. <u>Were</u> the grammar exercises easy?

(Page 59 Future Perfect Verb Tense) 1. see 2. will have finished 3. will have taught 4. wakes 5. will have arrived 6. will have had 7. will have paid 8. begins 9. will have driven 10. will have taken

(Page 60 Future Perfect/Negative Form) 1. It is not/isn't going to rain tomorrow. 2. The teachers are not/aren't going to have a meeting next week. 3. Robert will not/won't be studying geometry when his sister gets home. 4. Lisa will not/won't have finished her errands before her children get out of school. 5. Mark will not/won't have left the office by the time Marta gets back. 6. Ruby will not/won't help you. 7. Kay will not/won't have submitted her resignation before the new boss starts next month. 8. Dave is not/isn't going to receive the check next Friday. 9. The GED students will not/won't have studied fractions before they begin algebra. 10. Glenn's team is not/isn't going to win the next game.

(Page 61 Future Perfect/Questions Part I) 1. Yes, the weather will be cold tomorrow. 2. Yes, Candy will have saved enough money for a down payment by the time her husband returns from Iraq. 3. Yes, I am going to have a conference with my son's teacher next Monday. 4. Yes, I will close the door. 5. Yes, Luis will have completed his report by six o'clock. 6. Yes, Carmen will have had breakfast before she goes to the doctor. 7. Yes, the children will be playing in the driveway while their father fixes the garage door. 8. Yes, Nidia is going to work next Sunday. 9. Yes, the students will have received their certification before the teacher retires next year. 10. Yes, I will answer the phone.

(Page 61 Future Perfect/Questions Part II) 1. No, the weather will not/won't be cold tomorrow. 2. No, Candy will not/won't have saved enough money for a down payment by the time her husband returns from Iraq. 3. No, I am/I'm not going to have a conference with my son's teacher next Monday. 4. No, I will not/won't close the door. 5. No, Luis will not/won't have completed his report by six o'clock. 6. No, Carmen will not/won't have had breakfast before she goes to the doctor. 7. No, the children will not/won't be playing in the driveway while their father fixes the garage door. 8. No, Nidia is not/isn't going to work next Sunday. 9. No, the students will not/won't have received their certification before the teacher retires next year. 10. No, I will not/won't answer the phone.

Answer Key – Part I

(Page 63 Present Perfect to Present Perfect Progressive) 1. has been eating 2. has been studying 3. has been living 4. have been playing 5. have been practicing 6. has been taking 7. has been working 8. has been sitting 9. has been sleeping 10. have been arguing

(Page 64 Present Perfect Progressive vs. Present Perfect) 1. has been playing _or_ has played 2. has known 3. have been working _or_ have worked 4. has been 5. have been living _or_ have lived 6. has slept 7. has been raining 8. have been using _or_ have used 9. have been doing 10. has been taking _or_ has taken

(Page 65 Present Perfect Progressive/Negative Form) 1. Guadalupe is not/isn't absent today. 2. Emilio has not/hasn't been studying English for five years. 3. Maria does not/doesn't drive a red car. 4. Bertha has not/hasn't worked in a restaurant. 5. Mario is not/isn't drinking a cup of tea. 6. Hayde's wine club does not/doesn't meet every Saturday afternoon. 7. Cristela and Laura are not/aren't wearing blue jeans. 8. They have not/haven't been waiting since six o'clock. 9. Alma and Leidy are not/aren't angry with their teacher. 10. I have not/haven't been to Mexico City many times.

(Page 66 Present Perfect Progressive) 1. Mario has been working at the hospital for five years. 2. Mario has been working at the hospital since 2004. 3. I have been playing golf for twenty years. 4. I have been playing golf since 1989. 5. Bertha has been living in Texas for four years. 6. Bertha has been living in Texas since 2005. 7. They have been studying Japanese for six months. 8. They have been studying Japanese since November. 9. The dogs have been barking for one hour. 10. The dogs have been barking since 6:30.

(Page 68 Past Perfect Progressive) 1. had been feeling 2. had been waiting 3. had been working 4. had been surfing 5. had been daydreaming 6. had been fighting 7. had been running 8. had been playing 9. had been watching 10. had been studying

(Page 69 Past Perfect Progressive/Negative Form) 1. Chuck did not/didn't go to the dentist yesterday. 2. Terry had not/hadn't left the room when Chris entered. 3. Cindy was not/wasn't crying at the end of the movie. 4. I did not/didn't play baseball in high school. 5. Anthony and Duane had not/hadn't been wrestling for a few minutes when Duane broke his leg. 6. Alma was not/wasn't doing her math homework when her mother got home from the grocery store. 7. Lisa and Larry were not/weren't sick last night. 8. Gina did not/didn't take sociology in college. 9. Maria had not/hadn't eaten lunch when I called. 10. The mother did not/didn't put baby powder on her son's diaper rash.

Answer Key – Part I

(Page 70 Past Perfect Progressive/Questions) 1. Guadalupe's dress was pink. 2. No, Emilio did not/didn't attend class yesterday. 3. Wanda was scrubbing the toilet when I called. 4. My daughter's birthday party was last Saturday. 5. The engine had been running for one hour before the car ran out of gas. 6. The weather in Boston was cold and rainy. 7. Esperanza was wearing pink pants and a black sweater yesterday. 8. Yes, the repairman had fixed my refrigerator by the time I left for Florida. 9. My family had chicken fried steak, mashed potatoes, and green beans for dinner last night. 10. No, Margarita had not/hadn't made breakfast by the time Rafael woke up.

(Page 71 Past Perfect Progressive/Review) 1. take 2. swimming 3. before 4. had been dating 5. Dave was sick yesterday. _or_ Dave felt sick yesterday. 6. were 7. written 8. Had the couple been fighting for twenty minutes by the time the police arrived? 9. rode 10. come

(Page 72 Future Perfect Progressive Verb Tense) 1. will have been working 2. will have been sleeping 3. will have been living 4. will have been studying 5. will have been doing 6. will have been driving 7. will have been practicing 8. will have been taking 9. will have been weeding 10. will have been napping

(Page 73 Future Perfect vs. Future Perfect Progressive) 1. will have eaten 2. will have been saving 3. will have been repairing 4. will have finished 5. will have been teaching 6. will have been cleaning 7. will have been 8. will have done 9. will have been waiting 10. will have drunk.

(Page 75 Future Perfect Progressive/Review) 1. is going to 2. will have been teaching 3. are 4. is 5. begun 6. David have 7. is 8. next 9. while 10. won't

(Page 76 Verb Tense Review) 1. is sitting 2. studied 3. have seen 4. have been working _or_ have worked 5. will be sleeping 6. arrived 7. is going to fly 8. swims 9. were 10. had already left

(Page 84 Passive Voice) 1. My neighbor's house was destroyed by fire. 2. The book was taken by Robert from the table. 3. The chocolate flan will be eaten by Alexis. 4. The annual report has been finished by Bertha and Nora. 5. The tickets are going to be left by Mrs. Roberts at the front desk. 6. The purse snatcher was captured by the police. 7. The professor's lectures were attended by many students. 8. The export division is managed by Zoe. 9. The golf clubs were returned by Edward last night. 10. The mail is delivered by Al every morning.

(Page 85 Passive Voice/More Practice) 1. Poetry is written by Guillermo. 2. A magazine article is being written by Edgar. 3. Peter's homework has been finished by Greg. 4. The car accident was seen by many people. 5. The armored car was being protected by security guards. 6. Many children have been helped by Doctor Ramsey. 7. The surprise party will be planned by Araceli. 8. Free vaccines are going to be offered by the clinic. 9. The spider will have been eaten by the frog. 10. My order was brought by the waitress.

(Page 86 Passive Voice/Even More Practice) 1. Jack's car was stolen by a car thief. 2. Bob's car is going to be stolen by a car thief. 3. The last doughnut was eaten by Linda. 4. Two pieces of toast are eaten by Alex every morning. 5. Raw oysters have been eaten by Francisca many times. 6. The cup was broken by Randy. 7. Raquel's glasses are going to be broken by Vanessa. 8. The flute is being played by Maria. 9. This guitar has been played by Willie for sixteen years. 10. Professional baseball was played by women during World War II.

(Page 87 Passive Voice/Negative Form) 1. Children's books are not/aren't written by Sonya. 2. A letter is not/isn't being written by Mr. White. 3. The invitations have not/haven't been finished by Elsy. 4. The fight was not/wasn't seen by Cindy. 5. The apartment complex was not/wasn't being protected by a guard. 6. Many patients have not/haven't been seen by the doctor. 7. The party will not/won't be planned by Freddy. 8. The roads are not/aren't going to be fixed by the city. 9. The mouse will not/won't have been caught by the cat before we get home. 10. My glass is not/isn't being filled by the waiter.

(Page 88 Passive Voice/Questions) 1. Is a letter being written by Amy? 2. Was that house destroyed by a fire? 3. Will the cake be eaten by Walter? 4. Has the test been finished by Bert? 5. Had the budget been done by Maria when Magda returned from lunch? 6. Is the grass being cut by Paul? 7. Is the show going to be watched by millions of people? 8. Were the flowers left by Andrew? 9. Will the leftovers be eaten by Lou? 10. Was the book found by Blanca?

(Page 89 Passive to Active Voice) 1. Pat Dawson wrote that book. 2. Fire is destroying the building. 3. The enemy will capture the city. 4. Nanette had found the magazine. 5. Barbara has returned the tennis rackets. 6. Mr. Martin will sign the contract. 7. A Japanese company is going to build the road. 8. A bear was chasing Yolanda through the forest. 9. Andrea will cook the turkey tomorrow night. 10. The teacher is grading the tests.

Answer Key – Part II

(Page 90 Passive Voice to Active Voice) 1. Two floor fans cool the bedroom. 2. Cindy is vacuuming the carpet. 3. Julia and Ingrid are going to prepare tonight's dinner. 4. Have the students solved the math problems? 5. Andre was trimming the tree when he cut his hand. 6. The janitor did not/didn't empty the trash. 7. I will wash the dirty dishes. 8. Has Phillip opened the windows? 9. Hugo replaced the battery. 10. Marisa painted Amber's toenails.

(Page 91 Passive Voice) 1. No passive 2. I was interviewed by the program director. 3. No passive 4. Corn is grown by farmers in Iowa. 5. This house was built by John Ayers in 1932. 6. No passive 7. Was the living room painted by Mr. Sanchez? 8. The teacher's instructions were not/weren't followed by the students. 9. No passive 10. The dishes will have been washed by Elise by the time we finish eating.

(Page 93 Modal Auxiliaries/Can vs. Could) 1. can 2. could not/couldn't 3. cannot/can't 4. could not/couldn't 5. could 6. can 7. cannot/can't 8. Can 9. cannot/can't 10. could not/couldn't

(Page 94 Modal Auxiliaries/May vs. Must) 1. must 2. must 3. May 4. must 5. must 6. must 7. may 8. must 9. may 10. must

(Page 95 Modal Auxiliaries/Might vs. Should) 1. might 2. Should 3. should 4. might 5. should 6. might 7. should 8. might 9. should 10. might

(Page 96 Modal Auxiliaries/Will vs. Have To) 1. has to 2. have to 3. will 4. have to 5. will 6. will 7. have to 8. will 9. has to 10. will

(Page 97 Modal Auxiliaries/Have To vs. Must/Negative Form) 1. do not/don't have to 2. must not/mustn't 3. does not/doesn't have to 4. does not/doesn't have to 5. must not/mustn't 6. does not/doesn't have to 7. must not/mustn't 8. must not/mustn't 9. does not/doesn't have to 10. must not/mustn't

(Page 98 Modal Auxiliaries/Be Able To vs. Be Going To) 1. was able to 2. is going to 3. is going to 4. is/will be able to 5. is able to 6. is going to 7. will be able to 8. are going to 9. were able to 10. will be able to

(Page 99 Modal Auxiliaries/Review) 1. have to *or* must 2. could 3. should 4. might 5. can *or* is able to 6. will 7. has to *or* must 8. can *or* is able to 9. is going to 10. May

(Page 100 Modal Auxiliaries and Similar Expressions/Review) 1. Mario can work late tomorrow night. *Or* Mario will be able to work late tomorrow night. 2. It is past 11:30. I must go! 3. May I/we borrow the dictionary? 4. Patricia can finish the assignment tomorrow. 5. Matt is going to buy his first car next year. 6. He must go to the emergency room. *Or* He has to go to the emergency room. 7. She will come to class tomorrow. *Or* She is going to come to class tomorrow. 8. Drivers in Texas must have a driver's license and liability insurance. *Or* Drivers in Texas have to have a driver's license and liability insurance. 9. The weather in southeast Texas in July will be hot. *Or* The weather in southeast Texas in July is going to be hot. 10. Lorena was not/wasn't able to attend school yesterday because she was very ill.

(Page 102 Modal Auxiliaries/Would) 1. would have gone 2. would visit 3. would rather eat 4. <u>Would</u> you <u>pass</u> the salt, please? 5. would like 6. would rather study 7. would like 8. would have taken 9. would travel 10. <u>Would</u> you <u>bring</u> me the attendance report for April?

(Page 103 Modal Auxiliaries/Would/More Practice) 1. would rather be dancing 2. would play 3. would have told 4. <u>Would</u> you <u>take out</u> the garbage, please? 5. would like 6. would rather refinish 7. <u>Would</u> you <u>turn off</u> the air conditioner? 8. would like 9. would roam 10. would have visited

(Page 105 Modal Auxiliaries/Past Tense/Easy Version) 1. might/may have been 2. should not/shouldn't have eaten 3. was going to watch 4. had to leave 5. was able to help 6. was going to study 7. could have asked 8. were going to have 9. had to practice 10. could have talked

(Page 106 Modal Auxiliaries/Past Tense/Hard Version) 1. was not/wasn't able to finish 2. must have been 3. should/could have helped 4. had to wait 5. was going to wash 6. should have saved 7. may/might have eaten 8. must have liked 9. were not/weren't able to go 10. should have bought

(Page 108 Conditional Sentences) 1. owned 2. will give 3. had stopped 4. will buy 5. were 6. is 7. am 8. had listened 9. is 10. would get

(Page 109 More Conditional Sentences) 1. No 2. No 3. Yes 4. Yes 5. No 6. Yes 7. No 8. No 9. No 10. No

(Page 110 And More Conditional Sentences) 1. will be 2. would save 3. would not/wouldn't have purchased 4. will do 5. will send/sends 6. would buy 7. would have gotten 8. will look/look 9. would admit 10. would have become

(Page 112 Wish) 1. had 2. had gone 3. would tell 4. could have understood 5. were not/weren't going to go 6. were not/weren't living 7. could play 8. could afford 9. were not/weren't 10. had not/hadn't come

(Page 113 Wish/#2) 1. were 2. had gone 3. had studied 4. could sing 5. were wearing 6. were not/weren't 7. got 8. could have come 9. could attend 10. were not/weren't going to see

(Page 114 One More Wish) 1. could not/couldn't help 2. did not/didn't go 3. do not/don't have 4. am not 5. am not eating 6. cannot/can't speak 7. will not/won't learn 8. do not/don't have 9. am not going to retire 10. am not

(Page 115 Tag Questions/Negative Tag) 1. don't you 2. aren't they 3. didn't she 4. can't she 5. wasn't it 6. haven't they 7. shouldn't I 8. aren't they 9. doesn't he 10. isn't it

(Page 116 Tag Questions/Affirmative Tag) 1. does she 2. would he 3. did you 4. does he 5. will he 6. is he 7. do they 8. was he 9. has he 10. can she

(Page 117 Tag Questions/Review) 1. hasn't he 2. did she 3. isn't she 4. are they 5. doesn't she 6. does she 7. wasn't he 8. can I 9. hasn't he 10. do they

Answer Key – Part II

(Page 118 Too) 1. Lisa left right after lunch and Bill did too. 2. Dale is going to the concert and Betty is too. 3. Kate will be here at ten o'clock and I will too. 4. Shelly wants to go there and Herman does too. 5. My clock is fast and your clock is too. 6. Sonia is making progress and Luis is too. 7. Berry was arrested and his assistant was too. 8. Nancy will be there and her brother will too. 9. We go to the park every day and they do too. 10. Marc can speak French and Juanita can too.

(Page 119 So) 1. Lisa left right after lunch and so did Bill. 2. Dale is going to the concert and so is Betty. 3. Kate will be here at ten o'clock and so will I. 4. Shelly wants to go there and so does Herman. 5. My clock is fast and so is your clock. 6. Sonia is making progress and so is Luis. 7. Berry was arrested and so was his assistant. 8. Nancy will be there and so will her brother. 9. We go to the park every day and so do they. 10. Marc can speak French and so can Juanita.

(Page 120 Either) The first part doesn't change. Remove the comma, and make the appropriate changes to the second part. 1. and I didn't either. 2. and Bill won't either. 3. and Maria hasn't either. 4. and Daniel can't either. 5. and Brian couldn't either. 6. and we don't either. 7. and Erika shouldn't either. 8. and my answer isn't either. 9. and Barry couldn't either. 10. and Mr. Diaz wasn't either.

(Page 121 Neither) 1. and neither did I. 2. and neither will Bill. 3. and neither has Maria. 4. and neither can Daniel. 5. and neither could Brian. 6. and neither do we. 7. and neither should Erika. 8. and neither is my answer. 9. and neither could Barry. 10. and neither was Mr. Diaz.

(Page 122 Too, So, Either, Neither/Review) 1. Javier doesn't play tennis and Yolanda doesn't either. *Or* Javier doesn't play tennis and neither does Yolanda. 2. Ana didn't enjoy the play and her son didn't either. *Or* Ana didn't enjoy the play and neither did her son. 3. Delia saw the movie and Beth did too. *Or* Delia saw the movie and so did Beth. 4. Myrna hasn't been to Oregon and Jeff hasn't either. *Or* Myrna hasn't been to Oregon and neither has Jeff. 5. Pat should study for the test and Kate should too. *Or* Pat should study for the test and so should Kate. 6. Rosa does yoga every day and Lorena does too. *Or* Rosa does yoga every day and so does Lorena. 7. Paul has allergies and I do too. *Or* Paul has allergies and so do I. 8. Glenn can't drive a car and Elvira can't either. *Or* Glenn can't drive a car and neither can Elvira. 9. Dana wouldn't lie and Beatrice wouldn't either. *Or* Dana wouldn't lie and neither would Beatrice. 10. Craig is leaving and we are too. *Or* Craig is leaving and so are we.

(Page 123 Too, So, Either, Neither/Another Final Review) 1. Mario is working two jobs and so is Craig. 2. Vickie isn't married and Brenda isn't either. 3. Candelario works very hard and so does Luis. 4. My car hasn't been stolen and neither has Greg's car. 5. I missed the party and Vanessa did too. 6. Andrew doesn't like sushi and neither does Michelle. 7. Guillermina was absent yesterday and Theresa was too. 8. John was living in Utah last year and so were Bill and Avery. 9. The teacher has two children and so does Gloria. *Or* The teacher has two children and Gloria does too. 10. We won't go to San Antonio next weekend and they won't either.

Answer Key – Part II

(Page 124 Too, So, Either, Neither/Final Review) 1. Gracia is going to go to Mexico next month, and Oralia is going to go to Mexico next month. 2. Jesus doesn't drink soda in the morning, and Teri doesn't drink soda in the morning. 3. Marilyn is sixty one years old, and Thelma is sixty one years old. 4. Teresa can't speak Russian, and Lorena can't speak Russian. 5. Julian always runs three miles before work, and Magda always runs three miles before work. 6. I haven't talked to Melissa, and Ely hasn't talked to Melissa. 7. Diana won't listen to your advice, and Cecilia won't listen to your advice. 8. Jason loves to play tennis, and Rosalinda loves to play tennis. 9. My car is silver, and Patricia's car is silver. 10. Yolanda's hair is very pretty, and Ruth's hair is very pretty.

(Page 125 Too, So, Either, Neither/The Final, Final Review) 1. and Debbie does too. *Or* and so does Debbie. 2. and Linda is too. *Or* and so is Linda. 3. and Jimmy isn't either. *Or* and neither is Jimmy. 4. No change is possible because Brian and Keith live in different states. 5. and Cesar doesn't either. *Or* and neither does Cesar. 6. No change is possible because two different states are mentioned. 7. and Laura is too. *Or* and so is Laura. 8. No change is possible because one dog is big, and one dog is small. 9. and I do too. *Or* and so do I. 10. No change is possible because Adriana and Mariela drive two different kinds of vehicles.

(Page 126 Problem Verbs/Beat vs. Win) 1. beat 2. beats 3. won 4. will win *or* is going to win (prediction) 5. is winning 6. won 7. beat 8. have won 9. beat 10. beat

(Page 127 Problem Verbs/Borrow vs. Lend) 1. borrow 2. lend 3. borrowed 4. lent 5. Lend 6. borrows 7. has never lent 8. is going to borrow 9. borrows 10. lent

(Page 128 Problem Verbs/Do vs. Make) 1. does 2. do 3. make 4. has already done 5. made 6. made 7. did 8. makes 9. make 10. is making

(Page 129 Problem Verbs/Learn vs. Teach) 1. teach 2. learned 3. learned 4. taught 5. has taught 6. is learning 7. learned 8. has taught 9. learned 10. am going to learn

(Page 130 Problem Verbs/Speak vs. Talk) 1. talked 2. is talking 3. speaks 4. spoke 5. is talking 6. speaks 7. speaks 8. talks 9. is going to speak 10. doesn't speak

(Page 131 Problem Verbs/Review) 1. speaks 2. taught 3. has already done 4. Will you lend 5. beat 6. talks 7. learned 8. will win *or* is going to win (prediction) 9. makes 10. borrowed

(Page 134 Gerunds and Infinitives) 1. painting 2. to see 3. to wear 4. Swimming 5. to speak 6. to come 7. changing 8. fishing 9. to answer 10. finishing

(Page 135 Gerunds and Infinitives/#2) 1. taking *or* to take 2. watching *or* to watch 3. selling 4. to take care of 5. running *or* to run 6. smoking 7. working 8. playing *or* to play 9. to buy 10. to wait

(Page 136 Gerunds and Infinitives/#3) 1. watching 2. to move 3. to teach 4. to stop 5. skiing 6. waiting 7. listening *or* to listen 8. driving *or* to drive 9. to unload 10. reading

Answer Key – Part II

(Page 138 Gerunds and Infinitives/Forget, Regret, Remember, and Try) 1. receiving 2. to buy 3. to become 4. getting 5. to inform 6. scoring 7. to pay 8. putting 9. to close 10. to concentrate

(Page 139 Gerunds and Infinitives/Forget, Regret, Remember, and Try/#2) 1. telling 2. living 3. eating 4. to find 5. to take 6. to make 7. counting 8. to admit 9. to quit 10. spanking

(Page 140 Gerunds and Infinitives/Prefer) 1. receiving 2. waiting 3. to play 4. to mow 5. walking 6. to stay 7. driving 8. to fly 9. watching 10. to eat

(Page 141 Gerunds and Infinitives/Review) 1. to lock 2. talking 3. taking *or* to take 4. to leave 5. hunting 6. to watch 7. to see 8. to be 9. to save 10. to help

(Page 142 Participial Adjectives/ed vs. ing) 1. shocking 2. shocked 3. excited 4. exciting 5. surprised 6. surprising 7. embarrassing 8. embarrassed 9. confusing 10. confused

(Page 143 Participial Adjectives/#2) 1. frightened 2. frightening 3. annoying 4. annoyed 5. alarmed 6. alarming 7. depressing 8. depressed 9. relaxed 10. relaxing

(Page 144 Review) 1. The kitchen floor was swept by Veronica last night. 2. We have to/must take him to the emergency room. 3. If Clarence were younger, he would go to law school. 4. Lindsey wishes she had attended Ashley's graduation ceremony. 5. Natasha speaks Russian, doesn't she? 6. Maria left work at 4:30 and Juana did too. 7. Paul hasn't passed the test and neither has Alma. 8. They go shopping at the mall once a month. 9. My uncle taught me how to swim. 10. Young children are bored when they have to sit for a long time.

(Page 145 Final Review) 1. disappointed 2. fixed 3. will buy 4. could relax 5. is 6. was 7. hasn't 8. to tip 9. will beat/is going to beat (prediction) 10. exhausted

161